SECOND EDITION

42 Rules of Employee Engagement (2ⁿᵈ Edition)

A straightforward and fun look at what it takes to build a culture of engagement in business

Susan Stamm

Foreword by Curt Coffman

/UPER/taR press

E-mail: info@superstarpress.com
20660 Stevens Creek Blvd., Suite 210
Cupertino, CA 95014

Published by Super Star Press™, a Happy About® imprint
20660 Stevens Creek Blvd., Suite 210, Cupertino, CA 95014
http://42rules.com

2nd Edition: October 2012
1st Edition: June 2009
Paperback ISBN (2nd Edition): 978-1-60773-103-0 (1-60773-103-7)
Paperback ISBN (1st Edition): 978-0-9799428-8-4 (0-9799428-8-8)
eBook ISBN: 978-0-9799428-9-1 (0-9799428-9-6)
Place of Publication: Silicon Valley, California, USA
Library of Congress Number: 2009926405

Trademarks

Warning and Disclaimer

Endorsements

"Susan Stamm is a talented and engaging writer who offers personal experiences and business examples told in engaging stories and transforms them into 42 insightful action rules to encourage robust employee engagement actions."
David Zinger, Founder: The Employee Engagement Network

"42 Rules of Employee Engagement is a must have for anyone who is serious about employee engagement. Each "rule" is brought to life with real life illustrations and summarized with practical tips for implementation. I really enjoyed Susan's writing style—reminding me of many situations I have been in where it would have helped if I had this book. I also like the fact that you can pick it up and learn something of value in a few minutes by reading just one rule. This is one book you should keep on your desk."
Keith Ayers, Author: *Engagement Is Not Enough: You Need Passionate Employees to Achieve Your Dream*

"The 42 Rules of Employee Engagement delivers a straightforward explanation of the core principles that lie behind successful engagement programs. Easy to read and containing a large number of accessible anecdotes, Stamm's book provides the reader with a coherent introduction to the world of workplace engagement."
David Croston, Author: *Employee Engagement: The People First Approach to Building a Business*

"This book is engaging and inspiring. Full of rich stories and vignettes, it emphasizes the increasing need for leaders to help better engage their people in their work, and its outcomes. Susan's experience and competence in the field shines through."
Rob Fox, Author and Founder: Engaging Ideas

"As a masterful storyteller, Susan gives the reader what they need to apply the information immediately. This book is packed with 42 practical and powerful applications of engagement principles. When people are engaged in what they do, they will provide products and services to your customers in a way that keeps them coming back. Great job, Susan."
Stephanie Y. Oden, Author: *Ready, Set, Engage*®

"*Susan provides an excellent no-nonsense set of guidelines that managers at any level will appreciate. Most will say that they know this is important, but will agree that they often just forget to take these actions. Susan provides great reminders. She uses vivid examples from her own experience that make her points come alive. This is one book that you can open to any page, and tips and suggestions will just jump out!*"
Beverly Kaye & Sharon Jordan-Evans: Co-authors of Love 'Em or Lose 'Em: Getting Good People to Stay

"*Susan Stamm is right on the money when she says that "engagement begins and ends with leadership." Each one of her 42 Rules of Employee Engagement offers practical, action-able steps that you, as a leader, can implement right away to encourage the full and enthusiastic participation of everyone on your team. And in times like these, no organization can afford anything less!*"
Richard Hadden, Co-author, Contented Cows Moove Faster

"*42 Rules of Employee Engagement cuts through the clutter to offer quick, practical actions you can apply to boost perfor-mance. It's easy to get lost in the concept of employee engage-ment, but Stamm delivers the clarity and simplicity needed to find your way to an fully engaged team. Read it and reap the rewards!*"
Lee J. Colan, Ph.D., Author, Engaging the Hearts and Minds of All Your Employees

Dedication

To Rick (also affectionately known as "husband"): Your love has always lifted me to new places that I would not have discovered without you. Thanks for being my best friend, my mentor, and my partner in life and in business.

Acknowledgments

To Laura Lowell: your patience and insights have helped make this book possible. The tele-sessions, support, and overall great feedback provided to me throughout this process has walked me through my first book experience with relative ease and comfort—thank you!

To Charlotte Bris: your generosity in sharing your amazing editing gifts with me has contributed greatly to this work. I promise I now know the difference between crisis and crises, loose and lose, and then and than, although I may still be a little fuzzy on that last pairing. Thanks for the time you so willingly gave to this project. You are a wonderful friend as well as a talented editor, artist, and cook.

To Rick Stamm: not only for the encouragement along the way but for the hours of reading and rereading, editing and reediting. To be married to your best friend is a wonderful gift. But to be married to someone who challenges you to grow even when, or should I say especially when, you don't want to is very special. Thanks for always pushing me forward.

To Amy Blackwell: for helping me track down permissions and keeping me relatively calm. You are a wonderful detective and a talented partner. We are so glad you are on our team!

To Curt Coffman: your generously participating in this book still amazes me. Thank you for all that you do in the employee engagement arena and for role modeling the generous spirit and positive leadership traits that are central to building engaged teams.

To all the friends who encouraged me on this first book experience, in particular the members of the Red Rose Learning Community—thank you.

To Mom and Alan for being great parents and good friends. Thank you for being such positive role models.

Most importantly, to my children who have been my greatest teachers in this life, thank you for sharing your lives with me and for keeping me laughing along the way.

"In the end, an organization is nothing more than the collective capacity of its people to create value."

Lou Gerstner
Former chairman and CEO of IBM

Contents

Contents

Contents

Foreword by Curt Coffman

Author Christina Baldwin once remarked: "*change is the constant, the signal for rebirth, the egg of the Phoenix.*"[1]

While so many organizations, leaders, and managers seem to reach for change, very few embrace it and see the opportunity for creating value in their enterprises. A good case in point is how we view employees and our philosophy about increasing productivity and impact. Fifty years ago, more than 80% of all jobs were industrial, manufacturing-based positions. Thus, the true value of the human contribution was the person's hands and feet. The goal of managers and supervisors was to closely attend to (i.e., even babysit) every person to ensure they were doing what they were supposed to be doing, without interruption.

Frankly, we didn't hire human beings 50 years ago, we hired pairs of hands! The manager or supervisor possessed great power over the individual employee. If the employee did not do what they were supposed to be doing, the manager or supervisor would fire them and dramatically impact their families' financial security. The power base was clear—the employer did not need the employee as much as the employee depended upon the employer. Those days are now gone!

Today, less than 10% of all jobs in the United States are industrial, manufacturing-based jobs. This means more than 90% of all jobs require an employee to use their intelligence, instincts, and ideas as means of creating value for their companies. Clearly, the true value of today's human contribution lies squarely in the head and heart of every person. While the employer possessed tremendous power in the past, the balance of power has shifted and today the employee owns the means of production and creation of value. In essence, the employer now needs the employee more significantly than the other way around.

The new challenge is simple, "*how do I get people to do what I need them to do, when I have no power over them?*" Management struggles with how to adapt to the new realities of fully utilizing and energizing the human side of their enterprise. The key is no longer merely satisfying or attempting to keep employees pacified or without angst. It is tapping into the core values and beliefs inherent in every individual. Creating a passion, rather than just providing tasks, is the key.

Successful organizations of tomorrow will be those that've adopted a holistic approach to managing the human condition. People are messy, but this messiness segues to unbelievable opportunity for innovation, contribution, and lifelong commitment. The best description of what a workforce needs is "engagement," not satisfaction or job security. Engagement is the degree to which we are relating to our employees and demonstrating a true commitment to their development, self-awareness, and the willingness to transform the workplace one person at a time.

Susan Stamm understands these issues on a truly intimate level. She has studied, observed, and ascertained both a poignant and pragmatic view of how organizations everywhere can leverage the new realities of the workplace. Through her *42 Rules of Employee Engagement*, she outlines the issues facing both managers and employees on a daily and even an hourly basis. Her ability to see the need for structure where structure is resisted is remarkable. Unless your organization can fully automate sales, production, service, and follow-through, you need this book! Sure, many believe they have adapted to the new world of emotional economics, but from my consulting experience, they are merely adapting the old paradigm. I challenge you to take a hard look at yourself as you read through these pages.

Curt W. Coffman
Coauthor, *First Break all the Rules: What the World's Greatest Managers Do Differently*
(Simon & Schuster) and *Follow This Path: How the World's Greatest Organizations Drive Growth by Unleashing Human Potential* (Warner Books)

Have you ever hired someone who indicated very clearly on the job interview that they had little or no desire to participate in the work of your team? Not likely. You've probably never hired anyone who told you they planned to work hard at actively sabotaging your results either.

We hire employees who arrive on the job on that first day eager to make a contribution. They anticipate the good they can offer and the synergistic relationships they'll build within their new workplace. If that is so, why would so many people underperform on purpose after only a short period on the job? Why have engagement scores fallen to such low levels?[2]

Think of it this way. If your organization fits into the national norms for employee engagement, over half your team is not giving you what they could to help you achieve greater results. It is as if they take their talent, ideas, and experience, and place them in deep freeze while going through the motions of work. Why would anyone do this when work is central to our very identity? Naturally, we want to offer our best. It is this inner desire to give work our best effort that makes employee engagement the low hanging fruit of organizational performance. People want to be engaged, they really do.

This is good news because it is not large, complex issues that push engagement scores down. It is also bad news. Well sort of … you see, employee engagement has a lot to do with you and your style of management. It's those everyday challenges that wear away at the soul of your team: the manager does not mention appreciation of effort; there is no clear performance goal; no coaching or support is available; or, no one seems to listen. The list goes on and on. The result is that many employees leave to continue the search for the perfect workplace that will value their mind and spirit while others "quit and stay." Either action impacts the engagement level of your team.

This book responds to those day-to-day situations that seem to drive employees away from offering you their best. These ideas are not difficult to understand, but for some reason they are not common practice among many leaders. Each rule challenges you to take action immediately. Use these actions to transform your team. Meet with your team weekly over the next 42 weeks and discuss the implication of each rule for your workplace. Hold each other accountable to actions and goals that come from these discussions.

Specific tools are highlighted in a reference section at the end of this book, including a set of templates you can download to track the actions suggested in each rule. Another reference area describes some of my favorite books on this important topic. It is my hope you will embrace these rules and add your own to the discussion. A blog has been created for you to discuss these rules and share your own: http://www.tinyurl.com/chvthb (http://www.42rules.com/employeeengagement_blog/) I will look forward to meeting you there and hearing your contribution to this work.

Onward and Upward,
Susan Stamm
The TEAM Approach®
susan@teamapproach.com

1 Rules Are Meant to Be Broken

Sometimes organizations create policies for the masses the moment an individual employee (or customer) slips up.

To develop a fully engaged team, everyone in your organization needs to be a leader. This means the entire team needs to be able to exercise judgment on the day-to-day challenges and opportunities that present themselves. Whether or not this happens has a lot to do with your approach to managing.

Think about it. How can any organization win without everyone's full participation? Participation is a key indicator of engagement. In some organizations, however, rules, policies, and procedures are designed to cover every possible contingency so employees do not need to think or fully participate. Have you ever written to your Senator or Congressman and received a form letter response that barely addressed your concern? Have you ever complained about a product you've purchased and received what appeared to be a memorized response from an employee? Contrast this to IKEA,[3] where a prominent sign in their Philadelphia area store was used to recruit employees who would "think for themselves." This enlightened approach will attract top talent and build engagement.

Sometimes organizations create policies for the masses the moment an individual employee (or customer) slips up. Creating policies may seem easier than coaching and managing performance, but the results are dramatically different. When coaching, you clarify misunderstandings about performance and usually discover that few employees try to do poor quality work on purpose. Rules and policies are usually perceived by employees as an expectation of future poor performance—generally not the best way to build an engaged team.

Following memorized sequences and prescribed patterns such as "thank you for shopping at ...," is counter to a team approach which actively solicits the input, ideas, and good thinking from every member of the team. If your organization has rules, you may find that sometimes it is necessary to break a rule in order to provide extraordinary service or to go around a system that is not serving the customer. You and your team should actively discuss these rules to determine their impact on customers and desired results. By inviting discussions around rules and policies you send a message that sometimes the rule may not be the most effective approach. Such discussions increase engagement.

Shortly after our youngest daughter began dating, there was a surge in her text messages; but we did not discover this until our bill arrived from AT&T.[4] In addition to the monthly service for her phone, she had over $90 in text message charges above and beyond her monthly allotment. As we discussed this situation with our representative, we were surprised and delighted that she was empowered to remove the charge entirely and help us secure a plan that would prevent this from occurring in the future. True, AT&T was out our $90, but as new customers who had left another supplier only months before due to poor service, we were feeling really good about the new relationship. And, considering the long-term monthly increase in our fee, AT&T was not out anything at all. Yet the customer representative skillfully positioned the increase as a great service to us, which of course it was.

Yes, rules may be necessary, but they often prevent people from being actively engaged. Rules will never take the place of directly dealing with performance issues on your team. They certainly cannot replace excellent service skills and they should be scrutinized regularly to evaluate how they are helping to promote success for the team and organization as well as their impact on engagement.

Action: Make a list of all the rules and policies that are active in your organization for both employees and customers. Discuss these with your team and begin to analyze their impact. How are they serving employees, the customer, and the organization?

Rule

2 Get "Under New Management"

Think of "under new management" as an opportunity to try out changes that allow you to be open and upfront about what you are doing.

Today I passed a business with a sign prominently displaying the message: "under new management." Whenever I pass a business with such a sign, I begin to wonder about its intended outcome. It seems to be reaching out to all who pass by to say, "we've changed…come in and try us again, see how we have improved, we are really worth another look…"

What a great idea for team leaders too: "under new management." As managers, supervisors, and team leaders, we can provide new management techniques and approaches to those we serve by making changes in our management style. You may be one who boldly tries new approaches with your team regularly, or perhaps you are like many team leaders who are a bit more cautious about changing their style and approach. Change is uncomfortable for anyone, but under the watchful eye of our team members we can let our imaginations get the best of us: "What will they think of me? Will it come off as planned? What if it doesn't work?"

I once worked with a healthcare team that was in crises. As the group went around the table and shared concerns, it was obvious that the nurses did not perceive the physician as a caring person. One specific thing they challenged him with was that he never smiled at them or acted friendly. This physician operated from the "C dimension of behavior" (see Rule 18) and was quite reserved and task oriented in his approach. He seemed surprised by this feedback, however, and sincerely apologized to his team on the spot. Then he did an amazing thing—he made an immediate effort in the meeting to increase his affirming responses. As his team spoke, he smiled and appreciated their comments. To be honest, his smiles seemed forced and difficult for him, but his team rallied around him because he asked for their support and invited them to give him feedback any time in the future he was slipping up.

Think of "under new management" as an opportunity to try out changes that allow you to be open and upfront about what you are doing. A perfect time to put up the "under new management" banner is right after you have attended some training, gotten some feedback, or read a new book. Use these situations as an excuse to try new things. Get your team to support you. Openly announce that this is not comfortable or easy, but you believe it will make you more effective. Involve the team in a debriefing and get an even greater level of support from them. By showing your interest in their input and by allowing your direct reports to "coach" you, support and acceptance will come easier than expected.

Consider the benefits of taking the risk to try new behaviors and approaches and to involve your team in the process:

1. You are role modeling for your team the importance of trying new behaviors.
2. You are suggesting that improvement is always possible and that we can all work to be more effective.
3. You are involving your team and developing their observation skills and their ability to give feedback.
4. You are creating a learning culture.
5. You are growing and becoming more effective with each new skill you turn into a habit.
6. You are deepening trust and the relationship between you and the team by making yourself vulnerable.
7. You are modeling openness to feedback, a skill we all need to improve.

Action: Why not get started right now with this book? You can put up the "under new management" banner and seek support from your team right away. Follow the suggestions or ideas that are offered throughout this book and put your team under new management.

3 Begin at the Very Beginning

Imagine a candidate receiving a half-dozen personal notes in the mail from their future teammates.

"Let's start at the very beginning, a very good place to start…" The words Julie Andrews sang in *The Sound of Music*[5] turn out to be pretty good advice for engaging your team, too. I am talking about the place the relationship ultimately begins—the hiring process. Used strategically, the hiring process can offer an opportunity to begin the onboarding process[6] and evaluate the candidate for culture fit.

How often people are hired by the manager, or worse yet HR, and totally absent from the process is the team that will work alongside this new person. Taking this approach misses two great opportunities.

The first missed opportunity is with the team itself. They may be the biggest stakeholders in such a decision and yet they are totally divorced from the process. This not only sends a message that they do not have the skills to make this decision, but that they are not valued enough to participate in critical decisions that impact their team. So they watch and wait and rely on the "powers that be" to bring them a great teammate and hope for the best. But regardless of the end result, they are stuck with it. Being absent from a critical decision that affects them so deeply is not a path to engagement.

The second missed opportunity is with the candidate. Through the hiring process, the applicant can develop a sense of connection to the team and some excitement for the work of the team. She begins to see how she will fit in as a member. To accomplish this, the candidate needs some team time. Ideally, this time would extend beyond the team interview to include an opportunity to be in the work area for a period of time to feel the culture of the team and begin to build relationships and connections. The team can tap into the candidate's outside perspective by involving her in the team's work to see how it feels to work together and to help give the candidate a real sense for the work.

One local business in my community has taken this step very seriously. According to a senior trainer at this firm, this particular organization provides qualified applicants a full workday with pay in their call center environment as part of their hiring process. Such a day can provide a solid look at the job for the candidate and help to answer some of the job fit questions that are difficult to determine in an interview process. Members of the team are in a strong position to provide input after such a day and their observations can carry a lot of weight in the hiring process.

After an interview, a best practice is to follow up with a candidate. After all, the hiring organization is in a selling role and a talented, qualified applicant is likely looking at several options. This is another great opportunity for team participation. The team could send personal notes to qualified applicants to whom they will be making job offers, expressing their good wishes and appreciation. Imagine a candidate receiving a half-dozen personal notes in the mail from their future teammates. Whose employment offer are they going to accept? Begin at the very beginning by engaging your potential new hires during the hiring process. This team approach to hiring will also produce the highest quality hiring results.

Action: Meet with your team to discuss this idea. Consider some training on team hiring to help them participate in this important task effectively. Use DISC (see Rule 15) or another behavioral model with the team immediately after new team members join your team. It will help everyone get to know each other quickly and build connections on the team.

4 Listen, Listen, Listen

The 500 most commonly used words in the English language have an estimated 14,000 different meanings.

The first exercise of an interpersonal communication skills course I conduct for clients is a communication quiz which asks participants to choose their greatest communication challenge from a list provided. All of the selections relate to some form of speaking except one, which relates to listening. I have presented this program to thousands of people over the past 20 years and can report that about 2% of the participants choose listening as their greatest need. In the next activity, we read a story and follow it immediately with a listening quiz. Guess what the participants discover? Yup, they may actually have a few listening challenges.

Listening is central to our success at work as well as in our personal lives. It is the way we take in spoken and non-spoken information. We "listen" to body language and for what is "not said" in conversation. The spoken word can so easily be misunderstood. The 500 most commonly used words in the English language have an estimated 14,000 different meanings creating regular opportunities for miscommunications.

On a training assignment at a long-term healthcare agency, the first participant to arrive introduced herself to me as Sue, the "pool" nurse. As I was finishing set-up for my very first session of this organization-wide training initiative, I began thinking what a nice job it would be to sit in a lounge chair beside the pool all day watching the elderly residents relaxing. At the first break, I realized we needed to locate some backup restrooms when someone suggested there were more near the pool. Being unfamiliar with this building, I asked Sue, the "pool" nurse for directions, but she responded that she had no idea. I must have seemed visibly confused before saying, "I thought you said you were the 'pool' nurse." Well this produced a good bit of laughter from my class who quickly educated me on what a "pull" nurse[7] is and is not.

And so it goes. We talk and miss each other regularly in conversations. Sometimes communication "misses" progress straight to conflict. As a manager, you are in a position to listen for signs of communication breakdown and complete "misses." So if you see conflict brewing out of a communication miss, take action immediately by helping the team to clarify the communication. One technique that works very well is to have the receiver repeat what the speaker said, paraphrasing the speaker's thoughts *to the speaker's satisfaction*. Only after there is agreement that the communication has been understood, can the next speaker add his or her own comments. This cycle repeats until the team eventually produces understanding—people find common points of agreement they can build upon.

Listening shows care and concern for others and is a great tool to build engagement. Develop a listening culture on your team by role modeling good listening habits and showing people how to really hear each other.

Action: Get your whole team involved and committed to increasing their collective listening skills. Develop job aid cards that say, "Listen." Bring these to meetings and put them out in the open to remind everyone to listen. Keep one on your desk and be sure to place it in front of you when someone stops in to talk to you. Offer spontaneous listening tests (for fun) to help raise awareness. Ask others to do the same, but make it fun. Offer rubber wristbands to the team to snap when people catch themselves using poor listening habits. Let your team know you are working on listening skills and ask them to raise their hand whenever they are concerned you are not listening. Be patient with yourself as you are trying to work on this skill. Your commitment to work on this will encourage your team to do the same.

5 Be a Hands-On Manager

Silver bullets take a "hands-off" approach that allow the manager to pass off the problem to some piece of technology or to someone else.

We are all busy people. Problems pop into our lives without first calling for an appointment. Yet, as managers, problems "are" our work. I am not suggesting we alone must solve them, but we have responsibility for making sure they are solved. Working hands-on with our team to solve problems creates an opportunity to build engagement, but the use of silver bullet solutions often prevents this from happening.

It is hard to avoid the lure of a silver bullet when their abuse has become so widespread. One major abuse of silver bullets today is the overuse of technology. Whenever you place a call and wade through seven different menus you are experiencing a hands-off, silver bullet solution. The offending organization has successfully eliminated the "problem" of answering incoming calls, and perhaps has reduced costs; but does it create engagement? When customers finally reach the "live employee," how engaged does the employee feel when greeted by a succession of frustrated customers throughout the day? And then, of course, there is the customer…

It seems that technological silver bullets are pervasive today. As my son and I waited at the jewelry counter of a major discount retailer for a replacement watch battery, he gave me the details on why he had hated working there. He pointed to an electronic device on the counter and told me: "that was my manager." I was a bit confused until he explained that he carried this device around with him and did what "it" told him to do, complaining that some days it only provided about 4 hours of work for an 8-hour shift. He had no real manager to discuss things with and he felt frustrated by the lack of interest from, and connection with, the management team (if one existed).

Silver bullets are not exclusively technologically based. Let's take a look at my favorite magical solution: training. I usually become aware that I've been hired as a silver bullet when I discover that what I am training has nothing at all to do with the real problem. The participants in a silver bullet training session often have the distinction of knowing they have been labeled as "broken" and they have been sent to training to get "fixed." This can make for a "stimulating" learning environment.

In one such event, the manager told me that his employees were not being nice to the customers. After finding my trainees were rather passionate customer service representatives who cared deeply about the customer, we set out to define the real problem, brainstorming possible solutions (see Rule 33) to make things work better. The employees felt they had been heard (perhaps for the first time) and were energized about the possible ways they might move forward as a team. All that remained was to sell the manager who, sadly, felt he was too busy to sit in a training event and hear the concerns of his employees. Well, I was lucky that day to have found the manager open to what I shared and this story had a happy ending.

Silver bullets take a "hands-off" approach that allows the manager to pass off the problem to some piece of technology or to someone else. Yet, to build engagement with your team and with your customers, you need to be a hands-on manager. In the example above, the manager could have participated in the training process to build connection and greater relationship with his team. While he got the result, he distanced himself from the process and his team.

Action: Reflect on your personal and organizational use of silver bullets. How have they served the employee and the customer? Have they built stronger relationships and engagement? Is there a silver bullet you and your organization could give up? How might this impact customer satisfaction and employee engagement?

6 Be a Low-Tech Communicator

How often does someone approach you with a quick question and you are able to pull away from "your work" to really hear them and make space for them?

When I heard about an organization that had actually sent an e-mail to 400 of its employees to communicate that their jobs had been eliminated,[8] I began to realize how we substitute technology for conversations we should be having face to face. Just because we have access to technology does not mean we should always use it.

Today in the workplace the emerging standard for "dialogue" is the text message which uses the smallest fragments of communication possible to still convey some meaning. And yet, genuine dialogue offers the possibility of building relationships, understanding, and trust on the team and with the customer. Imagine how often rushed e-mails result in hurt feelings, conflicts, and errors in the course of our collective businesses each day? We need to unplug and begin having more face time with our team in order to build understanding and engagement.

Today, we are sending an estimated 62 billion e-mail messages each day. Do you suppose all this communication is building stronger team relationships and engagement, or further isolating us from each other and providing greater opportunity for errors and conflict? An e-mail was delivered into my box from an offsite colleague requesting handouts for a speaking engagement. After producing the beautiful full-color handout packets, I realized that I was only actually blind copied on the e-mail which was sent to "another" Susan at the client's location who had offered to run the handouts for us as part of the contracted fee. While I could have slowed down to notice the message was not to Susan Stamm (read about my D behavior in Rule 16), a phone conversation would have prevented this error entirely.

Consider the countless hours spent staring at your computer each day. How often does someone approach you with a quick question and you are able to pull away from "your work" to really hear them and make space for them? Imagine how new employees feel who need on-the-job coaching and support but sense you are too busy to really help. And, let's face it, with average retention rates in the United States around 2 years, many employees are still relatively new. There are numerous jobs that take at least that long just to develop proficient skills. I suspect much turnover may be related to a lack of support as the job is being learned.

For the youngest of us in the workplace, to avoid using technology would be unthinkable. Pat Noel, a corporate university director, and her colleagues at a regional bank, have observed young job candidates pausing in the middle of interviews to check incoming text messages, e-mails, and cell phone calls. This behavior from applicants with college degrees interested in climbing the corporate ladder is alarming, to say the least. However, a manager can hide in her office behind a computer all day long, avoiding connection with her team, but not incur any strange looks or concern. Yet, she may be every bit as dangerous to the organization as the person who does not know it is improper to send a text message during a job interview. Both sets of behaviors avoid human contact by hiding behind technology.

Engagement requires personal connection. It is a basic building block, an essential ingredient of an engaged team. How much face time are you giving your team? Increasing this time will be a large step toward increasing engagement.

Action: Discuss the impact of communication modes you choose with your team. Ask your team: Does meaningful dialogue happen here? Do we get beyond "task talk" and really hear each other? Are feelings ever ignored when discussing solutions? How can we increase face-to-face communication time when discussing issues on the team or connecting with our customers?

7 Everyone Needs Feedback

Our behavior has a direct impact on the engagement of our team, yet it is impossible for us to see ourselves as others see us.

Years back, a friend confronted me and told me that I was becoming a "bitter woman." At the time this feedback was offered, I actually was quite bitter but totally unaware of it. In fact, I had allowed some personal circumstances in my life to become so consuming that I was beginning to drive people away. But I was so preoccupied with myself that I never noticed. Many people must have seen this happening, but only one came forward—Peg. Are we still friends? I would trust her with my life. When people have cared about me, and have come forward with information about my behavior or performance, they have turned out to be the most significant of my friendships through this intimate sharing of feedback.

As a result of such experiences, I've often wondered why there is such a challenge with giving and receiving feedback in organizations. Why do we dread a 360-feedback[9] rollout? Many organizations say, "they are just not ready for 360 feedback." I believe what they really mean is, "they'll be ready when everyone will get a near perfect score." Do these organizations think that if feedback is unspoken concerns do not exist, or a lack of feedback will actually make them better? Surely, keeping the lid on concerns is not a path to engagement.

An even more puzzling concern has to do with those of us who have information to offer others that could help them grow, but do not offer it. In a formal feedback process we keep silent. We'd bristle at the idea of a face-to-face conversation to share this information, even when (or should I say especially when) the person is a close associate or our boss.

Holding back our observations, ideas, and concerns is not a team approach. Through our silence we are not offering each other or our organization the chance to be more or accomplish more. Do we believe that our feelings do not get communicated if we choose not to express them? By getting things out on the table, we can discuss perceptions, clear up concerns, and move toward greater levels of relationship.

Our behavior has a direct impact on the engagement of our team, yet it is impossible for us to see ourselves as others see us. We need input to make needed adjustments. When we invite feedback, we make ourselves a bit vulnerable; this is a powerful tool for building engagement.

My husband once suggested we are not really human beings, we are "humans becoming." Imagine the result if you could help your team incorporate the belief that everyone is on their own personal growth continuum that never ends. The important thing is not so much *where* you are, but rather that you are *growing* and making progress. To stop growing is the thing we must fear. Life and work are simply opportunities to make adjustments, but you need help in locating the adjustment points. That is where feedback comes in.

Action: Take one member of your team to lunch each week and ask for feedback on how you can become a better manager. Do team members feel you listen? Do they feel you are fair? Discuss the fear of giving and receiving feedback with your team. Express your sincere interest in getting feedback, and always thank the team for their input. Work to develop a healthy feedback culture on your team.

8 Keep Learning

> It is a silent behavior that says, "you owe me the right to keep doing my job with only the knowledge I arrived with when you hired me."

Imagine for a moment you are turning 16 again and you will soon have the legal right to a driver's license. To make this more exciting, imagine that as you anticipated this event, you had the foresight to save the money for a car as my husband Rick had done before he approached his 16th birthday. Wow, you are almost 16 and a car is within your reach! However, as the day is about to arrive, the *Encyclopedia Britannica*[10] people suddenly throw you a curve. A salesman visits your parents' home to tell you about the *Great Books of the Western World*.[11] All the world's best thoughts and writings in one set of books.

If you knew my husband as I do, you would know where I am going with this. Rick was in a quandary because he has always been a personal development junkie. After days of suffering over this decision, I am happy to report he was normal enough to go for the car.

My growing up experience was actually quite different. I attended a parochial school that did not even have a library until I reached the fourth grade. My town was a working class steel town where I witnessed the first signs of global competition. I watched my relatives lose their jobs during the steel mill's first ever layoff. The whole town seemed bitter and resentful. Most people felt they were entitled to an opportunity and, sadly, they seemed to be missing the bigger picture: mainly, that everything was in the midst of change. Everything that is, except them! They were unwilling to do the learning required to retool themselves for a new world that was unfolding around them.

Today we live in a time where the need to adapt to continuous change is pretty hard to miss. Change is everywhere and constant. Yet people often continue to operate from an entitlement perspective. They become complacent, which is a by-product of entitlement. One major indicator of complacency is an unwillingness to learn new things. It is a silent behavior that says, "you owe me the right to keep doing my job with only the knowledge I arrived with when you hired me." The really sad thing about this is that everyone loses: the employee, his team, and the organization.

A sure sign of an engaged team is an excitement for learning. The good news is that you, as a manager, can have a major impact on this. You begin by setting the tone with employees and helping them see the direct connection between their work performance and learning. Imagine what would happen if every employee was sent off to training after a conversation that sounded something like this: "Susan, we are really happy to be able to fund your attendance at this training so you may serve our organization in bigger ways. This training will sharpen your skills as a supervisor and help you build greater commitment on your team. It will help you reduce turnover and improve overall team performance: key requirements for moving up in our organization. We know you have the ability, which is why we are providing this opportunity. As your manager, I'd like to schedule a meeting with you immediately following this training to discuss the goals you set for yourself as a result of what you learn."

Learning is a key strategy for top performing organizations. As a manager, you can influence the commitment to learning by championing learning on your team (see Rule 2).

Action: The Internet is loaded with no-excuse, no-cost, developmental activities for you and your team. Try some today:

1. Free Team-building games and tips:
   http://www.businessballs.com/teambuilding.htm
2. Create synergy playing the colored business game:
   http://www.directivecommunication.com/teambuilding_idea_1.htm
3. Learn from authors as they discuss their leadership ideas and books: http://www.bookendsbookclub.net

9 Allow Your Team to Grow

We often find it difficult to let go in the workplace, especially when someone bestows that magical title of manager or supervisor upon us.

I was sitting in the living room when my 16-year-old daughter, with a newly acquired driver's license, walked in and explained that she was leaving to meet up with some friends. I looked up at her with the saddest look I could manage and said, "You're leaving me?" After a few quiet thoughtful moments, in which we surely did a role reversal, she calmly explained "Well, Mom, eventually." She then hugged me and left me to work it out on my own. My instinct was to hang on to her neck and not let go, just hold on there forever until they surgically removed my arms in some mental institution. Now, before you begin to diagnose my behavior too harshly, you must know that this was the youngest of my three children and the one that I almost lost in childbirth. She, of course, recovered and grew up without this event shaping her life in any way. Her mother, however, has never fully left the anxiety in the past where it obviously belongs.

So there I was, 16 years after saying hello to my daughter that very first time, being forced to face up to the inevitable—she was growing up quickly and time was not going to stop for a parent that could not let go. There comes a time in every person's life when they must discover who they are and what they can become. This is especially true in the workplace.

We often find it difficult to let go in the workplace, especially when someone bestows that magical title of manager or supervisor upon us. We suddenly feel responsible for "everything!" We want, as managers, to make so sure that what comes from our team meets our high standards that we sometimes find ourselves overseeing every detail of our team's work. We can suffocate our team this way. People can become resentful of us, feeling they are viewed as less than capable if left on their own to do a project. They may seek other opportunities where they feel they are trusted and respected for their own skills.

Why do we do this? Why is it so hard to draw the line between offering our support and encouragement and just plain taking over? How do we know when we have crossed the line? It seems we take over not so much out of distrust as over concern about the results. Perhaps we do not feel our team has the same commitment to the project as we do, and they will not give it the special attention we feel it requires. This seems to indicate a need to get buy-in (and assurances) before the project gets underway. If we meet with the team upfront to establish the priority of the project, and together lay out specific mile markers for achievement with a schedule of face-to-face monitoring meetings, we may find the confidence to stay out of the team's way and allow them to stretch their wings with this new task. Yes, it may not exactly match our way of doing things, but how will the team ever get the experience it needs, and build stronger skills, if we don't let go? And, if we continuously do the team's work, how are we to find time for higher-level tasks for which we have responsibility as a manager? Let go of your next project. Engage your team in it fully, monitor its progress, and watch your team grow!

Action: Have a team member facilitate the next meeting of a project launch. Provide a checklist of what needs to be accomplished. Attend the meeting but as a participant observer. Allow the team to learn from this new freedom from your control. Debrief the process at key points, but see yourself as a consultant or advisor and watch your team's engagement grow.

10 Support Team Members When Needed

It can happen to anyone, they insisted; yet it tends to provoke alienation and a lack of empathy from those who work around the person in trouble.

A while back, a story in our newspaper captured my interest. It was about a great whale swimming down the River Thames. It must have been quite a show as huge crowds of people were trying to view this enormous Bottle Nose Whale normally found only in the deep Northern Atlantic Ocean. The story went on to explain that the whale was likely in distress which had caused it to make its bizarre visit to London.

As you would hope and expect, elaborate plans were in the making to save this great creature. A whale in distress is something that touches our hearts and we want to do all that we possibly can. But are not humans also magnificent creatures worthy of saving in times of trouble? How often do we see employees on the job exhibiting somewhat bizarre behavior only to be greeted with criticism, reprimands, or worse yet, to be completely avoided and ignored? How often do we take the time to try and see these employees as potentially "in distress" and try to rally around them to help them return to the safe waters again?

I will never forget a particular group of employees I had the pleasure to work with at a manufacturing plant in Tennessee. We were completing a unit on the Attitude of Understanding when the group discussed the inevitability of having "a bad day." It can happen to anyone, they insisted; yet it tends to provoke alienation and a lack of empathy from those who work around the person in trouble. They insisted that this was exactly the time that an attitude of understanding was needed the most.

The team came up with a brilliant idea: the blue uniform. At this particular plant everyone wears white uniforms to reduce the separation and distinction between production and management. This group suggested that, upon hire, everyone could be issued one blue uniform that they could put on only when they were having a really bad day. This uniform would be a signal that they needed extra support this particular day. It would mean that they needed extra patience from their team and they especially needed care and concern from others. Instead of running the other way when people saw them, their teams would embrace them and help them get through their personal crisis and move on to a white uniform day. The approach would likely reengage most team members. Alienation, however, moves employees toward active disengagement.

Seeing unusual behavior as a sign of distress is a first step in helping employees through their crises and bringing them back to the team as a fully contributing member. But, whatever we imagine may be causing this behavior, all we really know for sure is that the behavior we are observing is unusual.

We must focus our discussions on the observed behavior, not our attitudes about what we believe may be at the root of the problem. In reaching out to engage a team member who may be in some kind of distress, highlight the behavior in question in a concerned and caring way and ask for her opinion. Your efforts will be returned with renewed loyalty and commitment to the team's work.

Action: Get your team together to discuss the inevitable bad day each member may encounter at some point. How would team members like to be treated on these days? Some may want "their space" while others may want encouragement. Discuss ways that team members can provide a signal to the others on the team so the team can spring into action.

11 Relationships Determine Results

He said the loyalty these employees demonstrated by getting results for their managers was in direct proportion to the relationship that existed between them.

I had the pleasure of facilitating a Leadership Academy for a group of excellent managers. This group had been so engaged in the learning process that the experience was just as enriching for the facilitation team as it was for the participants.

One of the concluding activities had the managers meet in mentor groups to discuss ways of increasing their effectiveness in various categories contained in their 360-feedback report. One of the areas they looked at was delegating. I listened in as a group took a critical look at this challenging skill to see what kind of ideas they would share with each other.

In previous cohorts, I sometimes heard frustration expressed over those few "problem employees" that just do not seem to want to work. Interestingly, whenever this would come up the focus was always on the employee, unless of course the focus would shift to the organization for systemic problems that were blamed for performance problems. But this discussion was very different.

One manager shared his observations on the secret to delegation with quite a lot of passion. He summed it up in one word: relationships. He shared personal stories of employees pulling their trucks in at 6:30 PM, well after normal quitting time, after finishing up a critical job and not logging the time because they knew it would reflect badly upon the supervisor. He said the loyalty these employees demonstrated by getting results for their managers was in direct proportion to the relationship that existed between them.

As I listened, I could not help but note the emphasis this manager placed upon what *he* did as being the key to successful motivation, team spirit, and performance. This was in stark contrast to other managers and supervisors who often placed responsibility entirely on their employees, or even the organization. It was never their fault when things were not going well.

I was reminded of a powerful lesson from AiA Classic™,[12] the program we began our company with 22 years ago. In one particular exercise, the author, Bob Conklin,[13] sums up the solution to all human relation problems in just three possible choices:

1. We can change our situation—change jobs, spouses, or living arrangements, etc.
2. We can change the person—make them act differently, make them work, etc.
3. We can change ourselves—alter our responses, our behavior, etc.

It was obvious that this manager instinctively understood what Conklin was suggesting. What we need to work on, of course, is really us. We are the key. Our relationships determine our results. Are you happy with the results your team is producing? Do you have the level of engagement you would like on your team? How might you be a factor in this? How can you begin to develop stronger relationships on your team?

Action: Meet with your team to introduce the three options for human relations problems. Have each person share how they have responded to the people problems in the past. Discuss how each situation might have played out had they used solution number three. What would have been needed to use it successfully? Keep these three options handy and refer to them the next time someone approaches you with a "people problem." You will find this to be a simple but powerful coaching tool.

12 Sharing Builds Community

Right outside your office are "real time" people that are hungry for connections that the workplace can fulfill.

When Rick and I were first married we lived in an old farmhouse that had been transformed into two large apartments. We shared a wonderful friendship with the upstairs couple from Maine spending many evenings together making meals, talking, and watching films. Each December, our friends would trek home to spend Christmas week with parents. Just before leaving, they would bring their Christmas tree downstairs to our apartment where we would enjoy it for the rest of the season.

Working in the Human Service Industry at this point in our careers, money was a real challenge for us. But there was something beyond the frugality of this act that was really spectacular. It was the stewardship of sharing a resource that seemed to catch my breath each time the tree arrived. It somehow seemed more special than any other tree we might buy just because it had been shared. It was an act of community.

I watch people struggle alone in the workplace and wonder why we are so individualistic. It is so counter to a team approach and our inner desire to be connected. Look at the Web 2.0 networking revolution: Facebook,[14] Linkedin,[15] and new communities that spring up each day with millions of members. But these are still "virtual" connections. Right outside your office are "real time" people that are hungry for connections that the workplace can fulfill. As their boss, your caring and community building is central to their experience in the workplace.

Regardless of whether we work for a big or small company, we all seem to be guilty of missing opportunities to connect with each other. A colleague of mine joked with me that she was unaware of something significant at work because her husband had failed to send her an e-mail. Her company has just two people in it, she and her husband. In our own little office we use IM[16] to send quick messages back and forth across the hallway. And, while it is terribly efficient, we must be sure we are not avoiding the opportunity to connect. We have to make it a point to have face-to-face conversations regularly to share critical information. Without a more personal connection we cannot share ideas, understand shifting priorities, or support each other—all essential ingredients for an engaged team.

How can you facilitate a greater sharing of resources on your team? Remember, getting your team involved in such a discussion is, in itself, an act of community. Does your team meet regularly now? How are best practices shared on your team? How can individual knowledge become collective knowledge?

Let's say you are reading this thinking: "Sharing? Well our team doesn't share much of anything." As one supervisor I worked with put it, "We keep our heads down and get our work done." Well, that may be fine if you are on a production line, but few of us do work that depends solely on us (even on production lines). It seems to me that sharing was one of the items covered in Robert Fulghum's classic book *All I Really Need to Know I Learned in Kindergarten.*[17] I guess a lot of us were absent during the lesson on sharing.

Action: If sharing is counter to your current culture, try easing into it. You might lunch together and share family news. As your team warms up, let sharing progress. Your role is to facilitate, not dominate or dictate sharing. Ask questions, listen, and appreciate contributions. Make it a goal to decrease the talking time you contribute at team gatherings. Keep adjusting your involvement downward. Ask someone to share highlights of a current project, or insights from a training program he or she just attended, or best practices that have been recently discovered on the team. Find out what team members are reading and how the team can benefit. Stay with this practice and watch engagement soar.

13 Your Beliefs Drive Results

As he put the plan in place, however, he found his team actually resisting his efforts.

Have you ever identified part of your work as difficult, unpleasant, or to be avoided? Have you held a belief about a team member that shapes all your interactions with them? Much of how we see our world and other people is actually a choice. I have seen an employee flourish under one manager who believed in her talent, yet fail under another manager who did not feel she had the capability to do the job. This would make a bit more sense if it were not for the fact that the work in both cases was the same.

In my own life, I've seen the power of belief illustrated again and again. Once, I was driving home in an old Datsun 310 with a quarter of a million miles on it. I'd loved that car even though it had parts falling off it regularly. One of its signs of old age was the way the heater worked in the winter (or should I say didn't work in the winter). In the exact spot each day of my 30-minute commute, the heater would begin to work allowing me to warm up just in time to arrive at my destination. I had memorized the place that I would be able to warm up on both the morning and afternoon trips and anticipated this as I traveled.

One day, as I pulled into my driveway at home, I was shocked to discover that my toasty warm car was only warm because I believed it was warm; the heater had never been turned on during this trip. I had been in deep thought driving home and had turned on my windshield wipers instead of the heater. As I parked and came out of my deep thought, I was curious about why the wipers were on and discovered the heat had never been turned on. It was only then that I realized that the car was really quite cold and that I had actually willed myself to warmth through my own belief.

Our beliefs really do shape our perceptions of reality, and often leave little room for other possibilities. This relates especially to our perceptions of the people we work with everyday as well as the work itself. I recall a manager I was coaching who had gotten a 360-feedback report suggesting his team saw his behavior as overly critical and analytical. In short, he was driving people away. However, he was completely committed to making changes, and we mapped out a plan for his new style of management and interaction. As he put this plan in place, he found his team actually resisting his efforts! We discovered they were not willing to see him in this new way. They were unwilling to accept that he could change and unwilling to believe his desire to change was genuine.

What do you believe about your team, about your role as manager and coach, and about the capabilities of each of your team members? These beliefs could be having a greater impact on results than you realize.

Action: Consider how your team's engagement might increase if you could see "people-management" as an exciting and fun part of your work. Write some affirmations[18] about this aspect of the job and repeat them to yourself to support your new belief. If you choose to see this part of your work in a positive way, you'll discover your ability to face any people management challenge with new surprising energy. You may also see a decrease in people management problems.

You're Still the Boss

What's the minimum percentage of decision-making authority leaders should maintain in any decision-making process?

This week I met with an executive leadership team that wanted to begin a developmental leadership process. A proposal containing 360 feedback had been delivered and the entire team was invited to come and discuss it before the process was to begin. One member of the leadership team raised concerns about past experiences with 360 feedback indicating he did not see value in what his direct reports thought about him. I found this comment both interesting and surprising, and suspected this leader was concerned about the feedback his team might offer him.

I was not prepared, however, for the CEO to shut down the process because of this manager's concern. I was even more surprised to learn that this manager's direct reports had recently complained to HR, indicating he portrayed a different side of himself to those he supervised than to his peers around the executive table.

Rule 9, you will recall, suggests it is important for you to let go so your team can grow. It has been well documented that employee involvement fuels engagement while providing numerous benefits to the organization. It is important to note, however, that even though you create engagement by getting the team involved, you are still the boss. If a project goes south, or if someone makes a decision that creates legal trouble, who is ultimately accountable? You are, of course. So how do you balance this idea of letting go with having enough personal involvement to be a responsible manager? In these types of situations, where you collaborate with a team member to reach a decision, you participate in a simple authority formula that looks like this:

% Team Leader Authority + % Team Member Authority = 100% Decision-Making Authority

In leadership workshops we often ask team leaders, "What's the minimum percentage of decision-making authority you should maintain in *any* decision-making process?" The answers range from 1% to 100%, with many suggesting that somewhere around 60% of the decision-making authority should stay with the team leader. The answer, however, is a little bit different:

Team Leader Minimum Amount of Authority = 51%

We suggest approaching decisions as equal partners while tucking the 1% veto power away, just in case it's needed. If the decision is not in the best interest of the organization, you use the 1%, carefully explaining to the team member (or team) why you must override the decision.

In my example above, the CEO, as the top leader of the organization, might have exercised his 1% veto power and suggested that the need to examine and develop leadership skills was central to the organization's success. This leader obviously deferred this decision to the team member. Did the leader engage his team? Maybe. Was this the best decision for the overall organization? Maybe not. Being the leader is never easy. Engaging your team means involving them as often as you can, but it does not diminish your responsibility for results. By reviewing outcomes regularly, and asking yourself how things would have worked if you had chosen another path, you can improve the quality of results while building a culture of teamwork and engagement.

Action: Reflect on the amount of authority you carry into the decision-making process. If it is significantly less than 51% you may be running a social club. If it is significantly more than 51% you may be running a dictatorship. Plan now to use the next opportunity to make an adjustment that brings more balance to you and your team's decision-making process.

15 Everyone's Not Like You... (Thank Goodness!)

If you are honest, you probably will admit that sometimes the way people approach tasks on your team has surprised or even frustrated you.

Why do people do the things they do, the way they do them? Does the person checking me out at the grocers ignore me just to be rude, or is she trying to meet her need to be accurate and careful in the checkout process? Does the teacher ignore the students' requests in order to intentionally frustrate them, or is he trying to meet his need to have control over decisions? Do I send unedited e-mails because I am sloppy, or is my need to take immediate action causing me to move too quickly?

If you are honest, you will probably admit that sometimes the way people approach tasks on your team has surprised or even frustrated you. Those same feelings quite likely exist for everyone on your team, because we each see the world and our work from our own unique perspective. Sometimes we feel that our way is the right way, or maybe the only way. These feelings can lead to disengagement on the team.

One way of understanding different behaviors we find in the workplace can be found in a model of behavior called DISC.[19] To get a quick fix on your most natural style, rank the four words going across each row. Choose '4' as your 'most like you choice' and '1' as your 'least like you choice.' Use the '2' and '3' ratings for the words remaining. Total the four columns to see which style (your highest score) is most comfortable for you:

D	I	S	C
Driven	Optimistic	Friendly	Careful
Persistent	Charming	Helpful	Detail oriented
Direct	Enthusiastic	Warm	Tactful
Focused	Influencing	Sincere	Analytical
Bold	Captivating	Caring	Precise
Self assured	Positive	Steady	Correct
Total_____	Total_____	Total_____	Total_____

If "D" was your highest score, we would call you Direct. The "D" person moves quickly to take action, likes to be in control, and is driven to produce results. Those drawing from this style have strong ego strength, enjoy challenges, and prefer to focus on tasks.

The "I" style stands for Interactive. These folks are far more focused on people than tasks. The most verbal of all four styles, the "I" person is a persuasive communicator and an eternal optimist who can easily persuade and influence others.

The "S" style stands for Steady. This style is very relational, but reserved. The "S" folks are loyal, patient, collaborative, and systematic organizers. They're also the most natural team players of the four behavioral styles.

The "C" style stands for Careful. A person drawing upon this approach will be very concerned with accuracy, quality, and doing things right. They like procedures and rules. They are analytical, task oriented, and reserved.

So whose approach is right? Perhaps that is the wrong question to ask. A better question would be: "How can we utilize the strengths of each style more effectively on our team while honoring and respecting the talents they each bring to the table?" The key to driving engagement is understanding and valuing all four of these work styles. As we begin to understand that others see the world a little differently, we can accept the fact that they approach situations in a way that meets their own behavioral needs.

Action: Learn more about DISC. Read rules 16-19. Download podcasts and hear DISC authors discuss their books on Bookends as they share their thoughts on this powerful model.[20]

http://www.bookendsbookclub.net/

16 Be Direct with People Who Value Results

For people with this D style, trust will flourish when a straightforward approach to communication is utilized.

Of the four work styles you can find on teams, one is known as the "D" style of behavior. This stands for Direct and is my predominant approach to interacting with others. These individuals are most engaged when they can exercise control over, and see the results of, their work. They generally have a healthy ego strength. Those exhibiting this style may come across strong and focused on results to such a degree that others may perceive them as uncaring.

A strength of this style is making quick decisions. This ability can be both a blessing and a curse. For me, it's a curse when I find myself hitting the SEND button before reading my first draft of an e-mail that really needed editing. Or when I've deleted a long voice mail message before hearing it through to the end where a client's home phone number was left for me to call. On the other hand, this ability has allowed me to process challenging problems quickly and swing into action while others around me may still be analyzing the situation.

To be effective with a person exhibiting this style of behavior, you need to take a direct approach in communicating with them. No beating around the bush. I will never forget an evening, about a year into our marriage, when my husband and I were having dinner. He quietly commented on the meal by saying "I really had no idea that there were so many dishes that included celery in the ingredients." This very non-direct style of communication is his specialty, and it comes from his "S" style (see Rule 17). Being newlyweds, I went easy on him (actually, I found it amusing). But, the "D" style wants you to say: "Hey, I hate celery. Great, and thank you for helping me understand you," says the D person. The "D" style knows what to do with this information…she only cooks with celery when angry with her mate.

One of the real values of understanding this style is in building trust on the team. For people with this "D" style, trust will flourish when a straightforward approach to communication is utilized. If you operate from one of the more reserved styles, such as the "S" (see Rule 17) or the "C" (see Rule 18) this will likely feel uncomfortable but it is exactly what the "D" wants and it is necessary for trust. This style does not want you to sugarcoat your feelings or catch you acting in a way that is not congruent with your words. This will break down trust. Not comfortable talking directly to the "D" style person? Tell him so. He will appreciate your honesty and the fact that you are working so hard to deliver information in a way that speaks to him.

In working to prepare a leadership event for a client with strong D behavior, I was told: "no fluffy stuff!" This presented a challenge for me because some of what my client perceives as fluffy I see as crucial interpersonal skill development. So I took some of the learning points I wanted to make and rather than use any experiential exercises, I designed a series of "fact-finding" exercises around interpersonal skills. The result was the same, but by packaging exercises as fact finding and data mining, it gave the event a more serious, business-like appearance. To engage team members or customers with this style, a bottom line approach is always a good strategy.

Action: Make a list of everyone on your team who exhibits strong ego strength, moves quickly to action, and speaks clearly and directly. Ask them how you can modify your approach to meet some of their behavioral needs. By meeting these needs, you'll increase motivation, trust, and engagement.

17 Be Enthusiastic with People Who Value Enthusiasm

Openness is essential to building trust with an "I" style person.

People exhibiting the "I" (interactive) work style are enthusiastic, verbal, and positive. Team members with this style will be most engaged if they have an opportunity for positive social contact. These folks are masters at communication and seem to have a real knack for putting a positive spin on things. They may break the ice in tense situations by cracking a joke and are not too fond of having to manage details. They tend to be "big- picture" people and often have a great many interests and friends. This may sometimes create time challenges as they try to balance all their "interesting priorities." Most importantly, people with this style want to be liked and accepted by others.

My son, Adam, and I both exhibit a fair amount of this style. Observing our family dynamics can be quite humorous at times. On one occasion, Rick, Adam, and our daughter, Sarah, were on our way to breakfast to plan a drive across the country. On the way there, we stopped at the Dollar Store so we might each pick up a notebook for planning and journaling during the trip (my husband's idea). We parked the van far back in the strip mall parking lot and walked toward the store, which was dark and closed as we arrived. Adam and I immediately turned around without a break in our conversation, and began to walk back to the van. When we got there, we realized that Rick and Sarah were not with us. We then discovered they were still back at the store trying to figure out "why" the store was not open. Adam and I had a good laugh at how important that information was to Rick and Sarah.

Rick and Sarah had a good laugh about how nonchalant Adam and I were, and at our lack of curiosity and analysis. Even though we had a good laugh, our deep respect for our differences has always enriched our family.

In the workplace, if we want to relate to a person with the "I" style of behavior, we need to be stimulating in our conversation and engage them in sharing their ideas and feelings with us. They prefer to interact with people who are a bit more like themselves: interactive, positive, verbal, big-picture oriented, and stimulating. They want to be involved in discussions and planning and problem solving, and want such processes to be opportunities for interaction on the team.

A client with strong "I" behavior invited me to a problem-solving meeting at her bank. When I arrived I saw she had created an elaborate tea party for her guests, complete with real china and cakes. The showy, fun approach was a perfect backdrop for the ideation session we were engaged in and was comfortable for this group of guests, each of whom had some "I" in their style. Had she invited the president of her company, however, he may have seen the trimmings as frivolous and unbusinesslike. Interestingly, she chose to leave this organization shortly after this wonderful event. Sometimes we instinctively feel our work style is at odds with the predominant work culture of the organizations we serve; yet for a fully engaged team, all work styles need to be honored and accepted.

Openness is essential for building trust with an "I" style person. This style seems to be keenly aware of times they are not getting the full picture. Withholding information and feelings will likely break down trust with this style who may view such behavior as a form of personal rejection.

Action: Make a list of those team members who exhibit strong verbal skills, are enthusiastic, and love interacting with others. Chances are these people have the "I" style as their preferred behavioral approach. Ask them how you can meet some of their behavioral needs to build trust and engagement on the team.

18 Be Accepting with People Who Value Sincerity

To build trust with the S style person, you need to be accepting toward everyone on the team.

People exhibiting the "S" work style are relational and reserved. This work style is most engaged in environments that are steady, cooperative, warm, calm, and collaborative. The person with this style is apt to be a good listener and a keeper of tradition. They may be slow to accept change and will likely exhibit great loyalty to their team, friends, and family. People with this style are warm and people oriented in their approach; they will work at a steady pace and make major contributions to the team and family through their methodical, systematic approach to getting things done. Most important to this style is achieving stability and accomplishing tasks through cooperation with others.

My husband, Rick, and son, Adam, both exhibit this style of behavior in their approach. The thoughtfulness and loyalty of this style has provided many wonderful moments in the life of our family. One day Adam came home from elementary school with a spelling test that had thirteen wrong. The paper had so much red ink on it I was afraid he may have been bleeding. Upon closer inspection, I gasped when I saw a note from his teacher. Adam just patted my knee and reassured me by saying "Don't worry about it Mom, it was a really good try." The instinct to calm people down, especially those of us who tend toward excitability, is one of the treasured traits of the "S" style. The idea that this was not the end, that learning spelling was something that he would plug away at and improve over time, illustrated the methodical nature of this style which can have such a calming effect on those of us with a strong sense of urgency.

The "S's" loyalty to their team and family is another wonderful trait. One evening, after we were first married, Rick could not locate me in our apartment until he discovered me sound asleep in bed. Operating from my "D" approach (see Rule 16), I went from point A to point B focusing on the next task, which was sleep. My husband, an "S" style, was hurt that I had not said goodnight before turning in. It was one of those early marriage opportunities to learn about each other.

The "S" style is an asset in the workplace and is often the glue that holds teams together with its relational, calm approach. The principal at our children's elementary school exhibited a strong S work style while living out Tom Peter's advice of "managing by wandering around."[21] He knew the names of every student in his school because he was a visible member of the school community. He was outside greeting students and seeing the busses off every day of his career. He made a fuss over anyone who retired from his school during his time at the helm, and celebrated special achievements the students earned as well. He'd be welcoming parents warmly at the door of any concert and shaking hands with everyone. His approach was not forceful or showy, just warm and approachable. Everyone seriously missed him when it was time for him to retire.

To build trust with the "S" style person, you need to be accepting toward everyone on the team. The welfare of the entire team concerns the "S" person and how you treat others and accept others will not go unnoticed by people with this style.

Action: Make a list of the members on your team who are calm, patient, loyal, steady, helpful, and good listeners. Chances are these are the members of the team exhibiting the "S" style of behavior. What can you do to develop a stronger relationship with them? Ask them how you can meet some of their behavioral needs to build greater trust and engagement on the team.

19 Be Reliable with People Who Value Quality

To increase engagement and trust with the C style person the key need is to be reliable.

The "C" style stands for Careful. This style is most engaged by results, but those results need to be "right." The "C" person will use time and restraint to be sure they get it perfect. They like to concentrate on details, to think analytically, and to perform a thorough analysis of work and projects they participate in. Most importantly, they would like their work to be perceived as accurate and of high quality.

My husband is a strong "C" style and his concern with my lack of attention to details has been a "point of interest" in our working relationship over the past 20 years in business together. One memorable discussion had to do with our checkbook. Rick seems to think that when you use a check from the checkbook you should enter the date of the transaction, indicate to whom the check was written, and record the amount of the transaction in the register. While I would agree these are all very important details, sometimes it is easy to get caught up in the excitement of the moment and forget to do these things. When I explained to Rick that the bank provides a statement each month to help you fill in these blanks, I could tell we had a different understanding of the purpose of a bank statement.

Early in our business when I was just getting comfortable with behavioral styles, I made a sales call in a high state of excitement about my ideas for this individual. I noticed my prospect had gotten quiet. It seemed that he was trying to move backward in his chair as if to escape. I immediately realized my "I" style (see Rule 17) had gone out of bounds and

I was scaring my "C" style prospect half to death. I worked to slow down my breathing and speaking and noticed an immediate improvement. Over time, I was able to build a relationship with this client resulting in significant business thanks to my ability to adjust and meet his needs.

On another occasion, while running a training event, a client approached me with a grave look causing me to think he hated the training and was about to fire us. He told me he had counted the coffee cups, and we were two cups short for the number of people in the room. I almost burst into laughter, but my knowledge of his "C" style was a reminder that this kind of detail was very important to him. I tracked down the hotel staff and had more cups delivered to our room as fast as they could bring them.

To increase engagement and trust with the "C" style person the key need is to be reliable. If you appear unreliable, if you show up late, if you do not meet a deadline, or if your data is wrong, you will find it very difficult to be trusted by the "C" style person.

Action: Make a list of the members of your team who have a strong need for accuracy, who need to be right, and who care deeply about quality and precision. These team members are likely operating from a "C" style and could benefit deeply from you providing them with the time to think things through so that they can produce a quality product. How else can you meet the needs of team members with this style? Ask them how you can support their need for quality and correctness.

20 Build Self-Esteem When Discussing Performance

This way, your team member does not feel you judging them, but rather supporting them as they try to learn from their good and bad experiences on the job.

A foundational skill of good leadership is to maintain the self-esteem of team members. This skill may very well be the cornerstone of good leadership but often leaders move too quickly to take the care needed to do this effectively. Anyone can be vulnerable to attacks on their self-esteem and lowered self-esteem is never conducive to being a fully engaged team member. Even the most accomplished among us can feel threatened when our view of self is shattered by others. A powerful example is found in the film about Beethoven[22] called *Immortal Beloved.*[23]

While the film has a fictional story line it offers a glimpse into the life of a musician facing deafness. In one scene, Beethoven is conducting his own composition but he is completely deaf. The orchestra is unaware of Beethoven's deafness and becomes completely frustrated and stops playing. The audience, also unaware of the problem, is quite entertained, roaring with laughter as Beethoven leaves the stage in humiliation. The film points out how easy it is for us to act on assumptions that may be totally off the mark and destroy self-esteem in the process.

Unfair assessments are all too common in the workplace. Joe had been at the bank just 2 days when told he was not following a procedure correctly. His manager publicly pointed out the error in such a way that was almost overbearing and then suggested it must be corrected immediately. As a new employee, Joe was enraged that his manager had overlooked his desire to do a great job while he was still working to learn the basics of the role. Joe ignored the manager's approach because he liked his coworkers and his work. The next time he needed some coaching from his boss, the same accusing tone accompanied a strong criticism of his performance. This time, Joe promptly quit.

Think of times performance has fallen short and you've confronted team members to discuss the challenge. Have you ever been wrong in your assessment of the situation? It is absolutely your role to help team members adjust their performance on your team. The best approach is often one that engages you as an interviewer trying to assist the team member in recapping the experience so they can learn from it. This way, your team member does not feel you judging them, but rather supporting them as they try to learn from their good and bad experiences on the job. By working to keep team members' self-esteem intact, you achieve greater results and maintain a positive relationship. It is helpful if you can develop a mindset that all employees desire to do the best possible job. Your beliefs about the employee's intentions will come through in your words and actions.

Begin by asking the team member for her opinion, and try to understand the situation from her perspective before providing your own observations. You may learn new information that enhances both the relationship and the performance of your employee. Remember, when you judge too quickly you can destroy the employee's self-esteem, and you could be wrong in your assessment.

Action: Pause the next time before responding to a performance problem, and think through your approach. Try to be supportive. Always assume the employee wanted a positive outcome. Open the session by appreciating the employee in some way before you move into questions about the performance issue. Make yourself a job aid card that says "listen" and place it on your lap where you can look at it often. Pause at the end of each answer the employee offers before speaking yourself. Often more information will be offered that will be significant. See each such session as an opportunity to grow your skills, your employees' skills, and their engagement within the team.

21

Involve to Engage

Caveman management leads to higher levels of turnover, disengaged teams, and poorer quality decisions

How often do team members bring ideas to you? Do you demonstrate interest in the team's input? Below are two organizations confronted with an identical problem, but the management culture produces some dramatically different results.

Organization #1

A team member notices an inefficiency in a work process and asks the supervisor to discuss it. Together, they plan to do a study of this process to gather data that can be taken to management. They complete an analysis, prepare a proposal with input from the entire team, and present their findings and recommendations to top management who implements their ideas. After just 1 year, management reports the new process has increased revenue by $500,000 and is eager to hear other ideas the team might offer.

Organization #2

An employee notices a work process that has some obvious inefficiency. The employee considers taking this discovery to his supervisor, but is reluctant about speaking up remembering the result the last time he made a suggestion. As the employee ponders the situation, he begins to feel frustrated, which he voices to team members who happily add their own concerns. The employee decides to be sick on Friday to try to lift his spirits with a long weekend. Two other employees must have had the same idea. The company pays for temps to keep things going. Having such a high ratio of temps on this particular team leads to a bit of confusion around key work processes and results in some significant customer errors. When the team leader is held responsible, the relationship between the team and the leader deteriorates further.

The lesson?

The impact of involving employees and seeing them as a valued part of your team can be huge. Often, managers complain about the extra time involvement takes. "We don't have time to discuss the best approach," says one manager, "I just make the call." This archaic approach to management should have gone out with the caveman...but sadly there are still plenty of "cavemen and cavewomen managers" out there. Caveman management leads to higher levels of turnover, disengaged teams, and poorer quality decisions. A lack of involvement will cost an organization lost opportunity and revenue, while the caveman managers are worried about a little time.

Beginning with the most frugal investment of time, even a caveman manager can get his team involved. Involve your team and benefit from their collective expertise, knowledge, and wisdom. As you see the return on the investment of your time, you may be inclined to invest even more time in the future.

Action: List decisions needing to be made, problems to be solved or ideas to be generated and pick one to give to your team. If you do not have time for a formal ideation meeting, post a flip chart in a central location for people to list ideas as they think of them. Host a 10-minute kick-off meeting explaining the situation and the need. Invite the team's involvement by posting their ideas as they think of them over the coming days. When the time is up, have each team member vote on their top three favorite ideas from those generated. Host a 15-minute wrap-up meeting to explain the results of the vote, and share which solution you'll implement on behalf of the team (or which approach the team will implement).

22 Use Your Head

Whatever your thoughts are, they are creating a blueprint for your life.

Bob Conklin, entrepreneur, author, and speaker, once suggested that you should "use your head to work for you, rather than against you." He said "The way you *use your head*, or think, will become the blueprint of your life."[24]

The idea that our thoughts create blueprints for our lives has been validated many times over in my lifetime. My father was a driving example of this idea. With no formal education, he found he had a gift for sales and servicing customers and always seemed to have a small yet successful business. These businesses, however, never really satisfied his larger financial dreams. He got this idea in his head that he would own a fast food franchise before he realized how hard it would be to accomplish this goal. When the leading franchiser in the industry took applications, Dad threw his hat in the ring. He became a top ten finalist out of 500 potential new franchisees competing for just five new stores. But when he was turned down because of the open-heart surgery he had had not long beforehand, he did not let this stop him from fulfilling his dream. He approached every other fast food franchise in the industry until securing a relationship with Burger King Corporation.[25] He immediately set a goal and began telling everyone he knew that he would own five Burger King restaurants and he got to work making this a reality. Not too many years later, at the time of his death, he owned six stores with his seventh store on the way. It is hard to say, had it not been for his illness, what he might have done next.

My friend, Bob Jackson, recently sent me a photocopy of an affirmation card he had composed during a program I facilitated back in 1999. At the time, he was in transition working two part-time jobs and was a bit down about locating the next right opportunity for himself. He had written a lofty affirmation about achieving "levels of success never perceived or understood before." As he shared this information with me, he was celebrating the release of his first book and preparing his dissertation for his doctoral degree. Bob somehow brought these affirmations into his conscious thinking and they became a reality in his life.

Cicero[26] said: "to think is to live." What are you thinking about today? Are you thinking that the job is full of problems and that they are going to be too difficult for you to solve? Or, that the customer will never buy? Or, maybe you see the people on your team as a bunch of poor performers that will never change? Or, do you look around and see endless opportunity, people eager to work with you, an organization open to your ideas and innovations? Whatever your thoughts are, they are creating a blueprint for your life. Be sure that it is a blueprint that you desire, because your thoughts do shape your reality. "As a man thinketh in his heart, so is he."[27]

Action: Tap into the head power on your team by meeting with each member to discuss goals and dreams. Find ways to support your team's goals through training opportunities, job shadowing, articles, and books. Encourage your team to learn every skill available through projects and tasks in your work area. At team meetings, discuss how the team's thinking is impacting its success. Get input on how the team can envision even greater results. Do a "head check" whenever the team experiences disappointing news or results and support each other in reframing the issue in a positive way.

23 You Don't Have to Be the Smartest Person in the Room

In fact, a sign of real genius, may be knowing when to share what you know, and when to put others in the limelight and keep silent.

Take a moment and allow this rule to wash over you. You do not have to be the smartest person in the room. How liberating for a manager who may feel the need to have all the answers, to recognize that this is not actually a requirement of the job. As a manager, you may be responsible for finding an answer, in fact you may be tasked with finding the very best possible answer, but having an infinite pool of knowledge and wisdom is usually not part of the job description. If you are feeling you have to have all the answers, you've done this to yourself.

Actually, when it comes to engagement, it is much better to *not* have all the answers. Have you ever had the pleasure of knowing anyone who had all the answers? Did you like this person very much, and were they liked and admired by others? You see my point. If you have all the answers, what can your team possibly contribute? When will there be a time for the team to showcase their creativity, ingenuity, and ideas?

Mary Ann Masarech, director of research and marketing at Blessing White,[28] shared a reflection about a great boss she had who always reminded her team that even if they were the smartest people in the room, they didn't have to demonstrate it. In fact, a sign of real genius may be knowing when to share what you know, and when to put others in the limelight and keep silent.

Many organizations I have worked with have a succession plan. This has always been a bit intriguing to me, as I have always wondered how people working in such close proximity would miss years of opportunity to coach and prepare others to take on their roles when the time came to do so. It is not that I am against a succession plan, it just seems that this should happen so naturally that a plan would not be necessary.

It seems that a lot of us work alone these days. We work in large companies, yet all alone. We feel the need to go it on our own and to be the smartest person in the room. And we feel that if we miss the mark, we are somehow just not good enough. We really could not be more wrong in our thinking; workplace engagement requires a team approach. People admire us for our imperfections, not our perfections. When we reveal our shortcomings and our need for support from our team, we allow them to connect with us on a human level. Don't be afraid to show your rough edges and be a bit vulnerable by letting people know you do not have all the answers. See if your team does not rally around you and become more committed to you in the process. Place people in the limelight whenever you can. Celebrate their great ideas and contributions. You'll see an immediate increase in these types of offers and you will find that many ideas offered are far superior to the approach you would have taken all alone.

Action: The next time a challenging problem arises on the team, call everyone together and admit you are not sure of the best approach to the difficult challenge. Get counsel from your team. When someone from the team comes to you with a problem, learn to first ask: "What do you think we should do?" Suggest you'd like to get the team's input before adding your own. Be sure to give credit to the team for their ideas. When meeting with your peers, be sure you are not dominating the ideation process or discussion. Create a seating chart on a sheet of paper and plot the flow of communication from one member to the next to be sure you are not dominating the discussion.

24 Compete with Your Competitors

Interestingly, many organizations use compliance to create what they call "a little friendly competition."

When one of the colleges in my hometown celebrated graduation, our newspaper covered a speech made by a vice president of one of the largest and most successful auto manufacturers in the world. This speaker related how, before going to work in the automotive industry, he had previously been hired by a large aerospace firm for a key role. But then this employer told him that his new position was actually already occupied. He was told by his manager to get in there and "fight it out" and the best person would win the position. He went on to say he thought this idea was pretty stupid and shared how, at his current company, they used all their resources to fight real competitors—the other automakers.

As managers, we tend to operate from a philosophy of either commitment or compliance. This philosophical mindset drives much of our behavior and interactions with our team, and may even spill over into our personal lives.

Compliance is all about control. With compliance we get exactly what we ask for, usually nothing more. We draw the mark and people perform right up to that standard, but seldom exceed it. With commitment, however, we get people wanting to make a contribution, to offer their creative best to the work or project. You usually cannot produce this kind of result from a management style built around a compliance mindset.

Interestingly, many organizations use compliance to create what they call "a little friendly competition."

Fortunately, few organizations take this as far as the aerospace example above, but too often internal competition is counterproductive to the desired results. Sales contests, production awards, and other incentives are just another form of compliance. These approaches put psychological caps on what people see as their endgame. Few break through these psychological mile markers to go on to even greater levels of possible performance. Another outcome of such an approach is the impact these contests and awards have on all those who fail to meet the grade. What do you suppose it does to those who do not hit the award level? Do you think it motivates them to try harder or increases their engagement on the team?

Never has there been a greater need to rally every last member of your team in a unified effort, ready to do battle with your real competition. Even though your team members have different strengths and talents, you need to be completely unified in this goal. The team itself is really key in harnessing this kind of commitment—and you are part of the team.

You can begin to tap the unlimited power of your team anytime you are ready to do so, regardless of past leadership mistakes or your team's challenging history. In working with teams for the last 22 years, we have found that an assessment of the team's overall performance is an excellent starting point. Such an assessment provides a snapshot of the team at that exact moment in time. The team then works together to interpret the results and chooses how it will move forward. It renews its commitment, heals old wounds, grieves for any losses, and begins anew. A key outcome of such a process is that it helps refocus the team away from internal squabbles and concerns toward the external needs of the customer.

Action: Ask team members to place their views of the team's top three strengths and top three concerns into a collection box. Meet with the team weekly for an hour (taking turns facilitating) to discuss how the team can further utilize its strengths to compensate for its limitations. Begin the process anew every 6 months continuing to meet weekly year round to discuss how the team is using its strengths to further its cause and meet its objectives.

25 Get Out of the Shower

I wondered what fears might be locking me into the "shower stalls" of my life.

One morning I got a bit more than expected as I took my shower. Looking down at the shower floor for the first time, I spied an enormous thousand-legger[29] trying to climb out of the shower. I knew "he" would never make it up the slippery fiberglass to his escape, but it was my escape that I was most worried about.

After letting out a high-pitched scream, I held onto the back wall of the shower as I tried to think through the situation. I knew that this creature was just as terrified as I was, especially after hearing my scream. Eventually my husband, who was out on the back patio enjoying coffee and the Sunday newspaper, would come up for his shower. I could surely stay alive until he arrived, couldn't I?

After a few minutes more of breathing and calming myself and not having any success at willing my husband to the bathroom, I decided to turn the water off. Immediately the thousand-legger moved a little, so I turned the water back on ignoring my concerns about water conservation in the middle of a draught. So there we stood, the creature and I, frozen in our collective states of panic both wondering, I am sure, how we would escape the situation.

As the minutes ticked by, I made the decision to make my exit. It took another few minutes to talk myself into it and then I leapt out, leaving the creature safely behind me in the slippery stall that he couldn't escape. It was amazing how easy it was to climb out of that shower! As I watched my husband capture the thousand-legger and carry him outside, I began to process the event and the paralyzing effect fears can have on our lives. I wondered what fears might be locking me into other "shower stalls" of my life and how, like this incident, they may actually be much easier to leap over than I have allowed myself to believe.

I began to think how managers miss opportunities to build engaged teams because they pull back out of fear. I remembered a manager I was coaching who described the terrible fear she had of having performance discussions with an employee because she was afraid the employee would dislike her and she would not know how to approach the conversation. Meanwhile, she became more distanced from this employee and developed anger toward her, because the employee was not meeting the "yet-to-be-discussed" performance expectations. In another case, a leader needed support to get his team through a terrible conflict that would have been much less severe had he not hidden from the situation for months because of his fear of getting involved in an emotionally charged situation.

I then recalled how terrified of standing in front of a group to present or facilitate I'd been when I first entered this profession. It gave me hope to reflect on fears I had overcome, realizing other fears could be conquered as well.

As I have worked with managers in training and coaching settings, many have confided fears that this role produces for them: the fear of loss of control, fear of failure, fear of being too open, fear of making a bad decision, and the fear of becoming too entangled with their teams. What self-imposed fears have been preventing engagement on your team?

Action: Examine your fears. Are they as scary as you've imagined? Make a list of each fear you harbor at work and at home. Next to each fear, list what the fear keeps you from doing or achieving. Consider the worst possible outcome should you face each of your fears? Which outcome is less desirable: the result of not facing the fear or the worst that could happen should you face the fear and not be successful?

26 Turf is for Stadiums, Not Teams

Turf wars get fed when managers dance around them and allow them to grow.

A common problem managers encounter in the workplace is interdepartmental conflict. Work groups and departments are always in a tremendous position to support the success of other teams for a larger corporate win, but this idea is totally lost when turf wars are in play.

Such was the case when the top management team of a hospital indicated the need for greater interdepartmental communication. It seemed that things had broken down to a point that committee meetings ended with nothing decided and top management would then rally to keep things going.

It was interesting to meet this top team that first time. They were weary and worn down to the point of being robotic. They had somehow allowed the turf wars to reach such a dangerous level that they had assumed much of the responsibility for operations. When our firm entered the picture they were working around 80 hours per week and had come to realize the connection between their behavior and the problem. They had successfully avoided dealing with the challenges caused by the strong personalities they supervised. Now their direct reports had more time to engage in turf wars which further accelerated their problems. The fact that this executive team thrived on challenge didn't help the situation. They seemed to enjoy the challenge of running the whole show and skillfully maneuvering around all the drama—at least for a short while.

Then suddenly a "real crisis" came along. I will define a "real crisis" the way most organizations define it: a serious financial concern, not a mere people problem that is destroying your life and turning you into a robot. There suddenly seemed to be a significant shortfall of funds to reach the end of the hospital's fiscal year. Our firm insisted that the executives hand the problem down to the directors and give them 48 hours to develop a plan. This would create an intense team-building exercise and serve as a reminder of their performance responsibilities to the organization. Because a pattern had been developing to do the bare minimum and let the executives fix it, we insisted the executive team explain their requirements for quality and completeness, and to communicate they would accept nothing less. It worked.

By insisting that these teams work together to produce a quality outcome and solve problems, they had to set their differences aside to get real work done. Yes, other things occurred here to help both the executive leaders and departmental leaders work through conflict, but the breakthrough came when the executives insisted the managers solve their own problems and held them accountable to performance expectations.

Turf wars are fed when managers dance around them and allow them to grow. I've observed managers carefully handpicking people for project teams based on who gets along with whom, rather than who has the talent. Allowing this kind of tension to go unchecked has serious consequences. Have you been running interference for work groups or teams in your organization that do not want to play well together? Stop. There is really only one team in any organization. Being in, and committed to, this team should be a prerequisite for continued employment anywhere.

Action: Twice a year host a "what brought us together" meeting. Discuss the overall goals of the organization and how your team fits in. Then develop a grid or chart that shows how the other departments in the organization contribute to the overall goals of the organization. Find out if there is any confusion about the purpose or work of other teams in your organization. Invite representatives from other teams to describe their work and key projects especially at those times when the need for cooperation and support from your team increases. Use this same approach for the individual roles on your team and ensure the team understands its critical interrelationship.

27 Right Actions Bring Engagement

When too much time goes into activities that do not produce results, I call this "playing work."

I once worked with someone on a sales team who would call prospects with the goal of "checking in" with them. He never set a goal to introduce a new solution, identify new needs, learn new information that could help position a potential solution, or concrete action of any kind. Consequently, he failed. While this was sad enough, the fact that this person had no direction in choosing how to invest his time for success was a bigger issue for management. Only people who could figure it out on their own succeeded. Those not lucky enough to figure it out fed the growing cycle of turnover, or became actively disengaged, costing the organization untold sums of money.

This scenario demonstrates a key need for managers to help people understand the difference between being activity-focused versus result-focused, and why it is critical that we invest our time in actions that move us toward results. In this example, the employee was busy, but his actions produced little results for the time invested.

This is becoming a fairly large problem in this information age we live in. A single e-mail today, for example, can end up taking a 15-minute block of time or longer just to understand the implications of the message and explore its relevance to our work. Few of us are aware of how much time goes into this kind of activity in the course of a week. When too much time goes into activities that do not produce results, I call this "playing work." One can appear to be working, and in fact may be quite busy, but his focus is on low potential or even time-wasting activities.

A great way to get a handle on this problem for you and for your team is to do a time study. It is a simple process in which all team members record what they are doing every 15 minutes over a period of 1 to 2 weeks. Just the process of doing such a study can have major payoffs by increasing awareness of where time is being wasted. Sometimes activities have a relationship to our results somewhere out in the future, but other more pressing actions may be needed right now to meet more demanding business objectives. As the leader, your role is to accomplish results through others. Such a process will help you stay on target for the results the organization is expecting from you. By using such a process you'll be sending a message to your team that results and right actions are what count on a winning team.

Action: After the team completes several days of personal time study, host a "town meeting" forum. You and the team can chart all the tasks that the team is investing in and together do some analysis. You can calculate how time is being applied and analyze whether or not time is being invested in things that tie directly to performance goals. This is a great way for everyone to get a handle on what is really happening and determine the efficacy of individual activities. Of course, such a process will work better if each member of the team already has SMART[30] (specific, measurable, attainable, realistic, and time-bound) performance goals in place.

28 Leave Your "Good Parenting" Skills at Home

Parenting, even good parenting, belongs at home, not in the workplace where it leads to disengaged team members.

Sometimes we can fall into the trap of becoming parental as managers. "Good parenting" styled managers are those who truly care and appreciate their team members, but tend to protect them from all of the unknown dangers "out there." This could take the form of resisting untried methods and ideas, or disallowing new roles or responsibilities team members want to take on.

Recently, I had an opportunity to meet with a friend whose organization had recently changed ownership. My colleague now reports to the CFO of the new parent company and was brining me up to date on her new organization. A little helpful background: my friend's organization is a specialty printing business which never produced its own printed product. It is primarily a call center. The new parent company had actually printed the specialty product prior to the acquisition of this organization. It seemed to me that the new owner would now have access to a large pool of new potential clients for its more traditional printing business by tapping the call center's customers. Knowing very little about the printing industry, however, I asked my colleague if the sales team at the call center would now have the ability to sell the more traditional printing products to their customers. She agreed that that would be highly desirable but then described how the call center had been largely ignored by the new parent company since the acquisition.

No one had offered to help the salespeople understand the basics of selling more traditional printing products. In fact, no one from the parent company was even working onsite at the call center. Months had gone by and my friend could see many such growth opportunities for the parent company, but her attempts to get permission to implement these ideas had not yet materialized. Meanwhile the niche specialty product sales were down and the call center team was feeling like orphans that were not understood or valued.

When I asked her to describe her new boss, she discussed his need for perfection and a high need to control the details. Yet, she indicated that his boss, the CEO, had expressed interest in his becoming more "strategic." She wanted to support this idea by assuming some of his duties and was really eager to do so, but he was holding the reigns tight. In this scenario, the good parent seemed to be saying "you're not ready to cross the street just yet. I can cross it faster and know the ins and outs of navigating the traffic, so just stay on the sidewalk, where you will be safe." The opportunity loss in a good parent situation can be just as significant as that in any bad parenting situation (see Rule 29).

The boss had justified his behavior based on the lack of experience of my friend. Examining the situation more closely, he might have discovered her aptitude for this work and also recognized her feelings of being under-utilized. If so, he might also have recognized that he could lose her if he did not acknowledge her need to grow and expand her skills. Parenting, even good parenting, belongs at home, not in the workplace where it leads to disengaged team members. Have you ever been a "good parent" with members of your team? Who are you holding back and why? How might your organization benefit if you stopped being a "good parent" and allowed people to take on new responsibilities?

Action: Make a list of every request to take on a new responsibility, or try a new approach or method you've received in the last 12 months. What percentage have you supported? Have you been a "good parent" type manager to your team? If so, it is time for you to allow your team to get off the sidewalk? Decide today you will begin to support some of these requests.

29 Leave Your "Bad Parenting" Skills at Home

Of course, there is no coronation involved in becoming a manager.

Of the two parental styles of management, "bad parent bosses" are the most memorable. Often, when describing a personal bad parent boss experience, people will accuse you of exaggerating because they say no one can really be that bad. They come in all forms, and at The TEAM Approach® we often get called in to coach them, sometimes as a last ditch effort.

I could describe a range of bad parent types, but the common denominator seems to be their poor interpersonal skill set. These are the very skills often referred to as "soft skills," but they are really the skills that make or break one's success. One manager we coached reached a level of notoriety that seldom occurs for bad parent managers: he actually made it into one of our nation's highest profile newspapers. The article said he ran his office like his own "personal fiefdom." Of course, there is no coronation involved in becoming a manager.

Perhaps we all have a tendency to fall into some type of parenting role from time to time, but when it controls us everyone loses. Unlike the "good parent" role (see Rule 28), which is often discreet, the "bad parent" role is usually out in the open. Even so, some "bad parent" managers are so good at the task component of their job that organizations allow them to stay while they create huge problems for their teams. I have watched organizations avoid taking action until turnover issues could no longer be ignored, or profitability had suffered. Eventually, if the manager does not do self-correction, most organizations will realize they must act.

As a manager, you will know when you are getting signals that suggest you have moved into a parenting role. Some of the clearest communication that occurs between humans is nonverbal. More often, words cause the confusion. When you pick up body language that indicates displeasure with a decision that you make, explore it with the person. Maybe your reasoning behind it is perfectly justified and you only need to present it so others have the benefit of what you know. However, if you are moving into a parenting role and your team catches you, you need to demonstrate real leadership and appreciate them for calling it to your attention and correct the situation immediately.

If you ever suddenly discover you've lost the ability to control your emotions or temper, no matter how you justify this, you need to stop and seek some immediate professional support. Find a coach, and consider tapping into your organization's EAP[31] program if one is available. Some health insurance plans provide a specified number of therapeutic sessions per year that will allow you to work with a mental health professional. Anyone can fall into mild depression, which can affect relationships more intensely than we often realize. Some people today still feel stigmatized by needing this kind of support. Don't allow that kind of thinking to stop you from getting what you need. Your career, happiness, and even health could be at risk. This behavior, if left unchecked, can spill over into your home life and begin to poison relationships with the people you care about the most. Get support right away and allow yourself to move on to the emotionally healthy, mature person that is within.

Action: Gather examples from your friends and associates of the scariest possible behaviors a manager could ever exhibit. These would be a list of "bad parent" manager behaviors. Use this list to do an honest self-assessment and if you find you need help, get it. For those who pass the test, take your employees to lunch individually and ask for straightforward feedback on one behavior they would like to see you change. Take notes. Be sure to thank them and report back with your personal plan. Meet regularly to ask for their perceptions of your progress.

30 Expect Exceeded Expectations

Why is it so hard for us to just give people the benefit of the doubt and always assume they are capable of more?

In my very first job out of college, I met a woman who had been a cruel victim of the perceptions of people around her. At the time, I was working at a state institution with people who had developmental disabilities and had been institutionalized since birth. It was assumed that the woman in question was profoundly developmentally disabled along with her extreme physical disabilities because she had no way of relaying her thoughts through speech. Just 2 years before I met her, a speech therapist began to work with her and discovered that not only was she *not* developmentally disabled, but she was, in fact, a quite intelligent high functioning individual. She had lived isolated from any family for 30 years of her life warehoused with other forgotten people. Staff members had spoken to her as if she had little or no understanding of her surroundings and she had little to stimulate her active intelligent mind until the magical day that the discovery was made.

Truly, we can never really know what is inside another person, what they are capable of, and what past circumstances contributed to who they are today. Sometimes painful memories and experiences bring people back to places that make it difficult for them to show others their very best selves. I sometimes revert to that moment when I was escorted from my first grade desk to the office by Sister Saint Dorothy. There I found my mother waiting in the office of the small school. As the news of my "mental retardation" was shared with my mother

I remember thinking that there was something terribly wrong with me, and how sorry I was to disappoint my mother this way. Dyslexia[32] was an unknown problem back in the early sixties when the nun made her diagnosis, but the impact of her innocent incompetence has provided many opportunities for me to work on my own self-esteem throughout my life.

Why is it so hard for us to just give people the benefit of the doubt and always assume they are capable of more? Is this not the key role of being a manager: to help others grow and reach their potential? By expecting more and greater things from our team members, we challenge them to grow and we engage them more intensely in their work.

What would happen if we always chose to believe our employees have "it" somewhere within them, and our role is to help them locate it? I am not just talking about your top performers; I am also talking about your bottom performers. Have you increased your expectations of these team members lately or expressed your confidence in them? Who might they become if they just had someone who would believe in them, encourage them, and mentor them? Being underutilized is a key reason employees leave organizations today. Are your team members challenged enough?

Action: Here is a challenge for you to try: pretend your team has ten times more capability than you are currently utilizing. How might this knowledge impact your relationships with them and your conversations over the next weeks and months? What challenges can you give them to tackle, what ideas can you pump them for, how can your organization benefit from this untapped potential?

31 | It Only Takes a Minute

In fact, a large number of people who call themselves managers appear to invest very little time in their teams whatsoever until there is a crisis.

Do you suppose that in the course of your day you ever waste a minute? How about 5 minutes? Is it possible that you might actually misuse 30 minutes during the course of a single day? According to Steve Pavlina,[33] the average employee misuses enormous amounts of time. "The average full-time worker doesn't even start doing real work until 11:00 a.m.," Steve writes, "and begins to wind down around 3:30 p.m." But if you are reading this book, let's assume you're a high performer and you only underutilize 30 minutes of time, on average, 3 days per week. This provides you with 1.5 hours a week you could invest in developing your team without losing any of your current personal productivity.

Managers often operate from the illusion that it will take large amounts of time (certainly more than they have available) to mentor, coach, and develop talent in their teams. Consequently, a great many managers ignore opportunities to improve performance altogether. In fact, a large number of people who call themselves managers appear to invest very little time in their teams whatsoever until there is a crisis. It seems that these individuals are not managers at all; they are actually highly paid individual contributors who become "crisis managers" when emergencies arise.

Back in the eighties, a timeless little book challenged conventional wisdom that good management takes a lot of time. It presented a revolutionary idea that a manager could address key performance needs in "a minute." The book I am referring to, of course, is the *One Minute Manager* by Ken Blanchard.[34] The concept of "one minute" in this book is symbolic of the small amount of time these critically important activities actually require.

At The TEAM Approach®, we work with managers and supervisors to help them utilize "coaching moments." These brief coaching sessions utilize an "interview style approach" instead of a "telling style approach" to help employees learn from their experiences (see Rule 41). We encourage managers to take some time to be visible by just hanging around their teams observing and supporting the team's work. They find plenty of opportunities for coaching moments when they take the time to be more present in the work of their team. These informal coaching opportunities can happen quickly and spontaneously on the spot. Occasionally, a need for coaching moments will be brought to a manager by a team member. Some of these situations may require a more formal meeting. But most coaching opportunities do not need to take large amounts of time or even a sit-down appointment.

Time is available right now to support your team in key ways that will contribute to improved performance and results. Do you remember the Hawthorn Studies?[35] We've known for decades that just by increasing your personal interest in your team you will also increase engagement on your team. We can always find the time, somehow, to fix the inevitable results that poor performance brings. Why not be proactive and develop your team up front—it takes less time, is less stressful, and positions you as a more competent, proactive leader.

Action: Begin by making a commitment to step away from your desk and observe, interact, and learn more about the challenges your team faces every day. Develop the habit of doing this once a day, or at least a few times per week. Find regular opportunities to reinforce the kind of behavior that gets results. Meet with staff regularly to discuss goals and priorities and to get input on progress so you're in a better position to recognize good performance (see Rule 32).

32 Recognize Good Performances

I believe many managers do not distinguish between their personal feelings of appreciation and the actual act of communicating appreciation and recognition.

How do you think each of your employees would rate you on your frequency of praising their good performance? Who on the team would rate you the highest? Who would rate you the lowest, and why would a discrepancy exist?

Based on surveys administered by The TEAM Approach® to a wide range of organizations over our 22-year history, the single-most consistent concern raised by employees is a "lack of recognition for a job well done." Managers are always surprised by this and I really believe many managers do not distinguish between their personal feelings of appreciation and the actual act of communicating appreciation and recognition. They "assume" employees know how they feel about their good work and contributions. They do not.

In my first professional job out of college, I was working as a human service worker with people who were developmentally disabled. We set up formal reinforcement schedules using a 6 to 1 ratio to shape the behavior we desired, making sure we always offered six positive reinforcements for good behavior before offering any critical feedback.

Surely this schedule was needed for this particular population. But even in the workplace, the idea of "earning the right" to give someone critical feedback holds true. In Kim Cameron's new book, *Positive Leadership*,[36] he shares his research that found "the single most important factor in producing organizational performance was the ratio of positive statements to negative statements." By providing recognition for great performance, you are also earning the right to provide performance coaching when performance misses the mark. On the other hand, if employees only ever get feedback when performance falls short, it is likely they will not value that feedback.

Sometimes organizational systems for recognizing people are so "standardized" they lose all meaning and impact. Managers may misuse these systems as a "silver bullet" for all their employee recognition needs (see Rule 5). Employee of the Month and Year programs are fine if they are not used as replacements for the most critical kind of recognition—that which comes from the immediate supervisor personally recognizing good performance. I have seen organizations create standardized recognition programs and then work to spread the recognition around so it is perceived as "fair." These organizations actually think employees are not on to the contrived way such systems actually work.

A participant in a training session once shared an unbelievable story with our class. When he celebrated his 30-year anniversary working for a federal agency, no party, balloon, or card marked this event. Instead, he found a "form post card" in his mailbox at his home. On the typeset card he read: "Thank you for your ___ years of service" and the number 30 had been written in on the card. He shared with both sadness and anger that he would have preferred that his employer had ignored the event entirely.

What could be more simple than telling someone we appreciate his or her work? Perhaps that is the problem, it is so simple it gets overlooked. Don't let the simplicity of this act fool you. It is a powerful tool for engaging your team and will go a long way toward retaining talent.

Action: For the next 3 days try taking the "penny challenge." In the morning, before coming to work, place ten pennies in your left pocket. Each time you provide a word of "sincere positive feedback" to one of your employees move one penny to the right pocket. At the end of the day, you have a measure of how much praise you are really providing. Try to increase your praise score by at least one each day, especially with your direct reports. And remember, your peers and boss are also hungry for some positive words. Just one person working consistently at this can create a new trend in your organization's recognition culture.

33 Problem Solving Is a Team Sport

Too often problems are defined in the proverbial "ivory tower," far away from those who know the weak links in the process.

Employees who've developed problem solving skills, and are invited to participate in the process, are more likely to be engaged than those who get solutions handed to them. The following steps will provide a sound process to engage your team in problem solving.

Step One: Define the Problem. In the rush to stop the bleed, many people skip this first, most critical step. Let's say sales are down. Any number of reasons could be at play: the product has outlived its usefulness, sales associates lack skill, the marketing message is not getting above the noise, customer service has been disappointing, etc. This first step of the problem-solving process points us in the direction of a solution. Getting everyone on the team connected to the problem helps assure success in this step. Too often problems are defined in the proverbial "ivory tower" far away from those who know the weak links in the process. Brainstorming (Step 3) is a useful tool for getting input on all the possible definitions for a problem.

Step Two: Gather Facts and Data. Today we have the power of the Internet to research news and statistics that relate to our problem, or to research similar scenarios that might help us. By getting the team involved in fact gathering, you are building buy-in for the direction that will ultimately be taken to solve the problem. Your team can host interviews with key stakeholders, research data, and be far more effective utilizing a team approach to fact gathering than a single manager could ever hope to be. This step in the process will build skills and engagement in the team.

Step Three: Brainstorm Solutions. Many times teams violate the fundamental rules of this activity. Poor brainstorming practices can shut down the creative process and disengage your team. Post the brainstorming rules so that all can be reminded of them during this step. The first rule is to go for "quantity not quality." A second rule is to "withhold judgment" which is necessary for the first rule to be successful. As the team brainstorms, write the ideas on a white board or flip chart so all can see them. This allows people to combine and blend different ideas together (hitch-hiking ideas) for new and creative solutions.

Step Four: Pick the Best Solution. Drawing from all your data and understanding of the situation gathered in Step 2, you should now be in a position to select the solution best suited to your problem. Many decision-making tools can aid your team at this stage of the process. One of my personal favorites is called "pit the pairs." You'll find instruc-tions for this activity on our Web site:
http://www.teamapproach.com/42rulesresources.asp

Step Five: Implement the Solution. This is the action step. Give your solution a fair try.

Step Six: Evaluate the Result. When you have reached the agreed-upon time or measurement, check to see how your solution is working and decide if it is still viable. If not, return to Step 1 and walk through the process again making sure you have not missed anything in your definition, fact gathering, etc. Find a new solution to implement and repeat the evaluation step at the appropriate time.

Action: Practice brainstorming to help your team learn the rules. Use simple things around the office: paper clips, pencils, trash can, etc., as objects for this activity. Divide your team into groups of three and assign an object to each group. Give them a few minutes time to create a list of possible uses for the item on a white board or flip chart. See which group comes up with the most creative ideas in the time allowed. Debrief asking if anyone tried to block an idea during the process. Use this as a warm up before tackling a real problem on the team.

34 Help Your Team Accept Change

Skills, aptitude, and talent for the work should be considered when making changes just as if you were hiring a new employee for a position.

Change seems to be everywhere, but does your team readily embrace and support critical changes? Many times change is not positioned effectively in the workplace. Employees may feel like victims of change, disempowered and without any control. A few key elements will support engagement in your team while driving needed change.

A wise proverb suggests: "Where there is no vision, the people perish."[37] Well, your employees may not perish, but without vision they may not embrace or champion the change. Do your employees understand your organization's overall vision, the team's vision, and the vision for change? Seeing a bigger picture can promote stronger engagement and support for the change. A well-known story is told of a NASA janitor who was asked by a visitor what he was doing, to which he responded, "I'm putting a man on the moon."[38] Vision connects us to our work and helps us accept change.

After vision, your team needs sufficient skill to implement changes. I once worked with a food manufacturer who had a sudden idea to turn their internal customer service team into a sales team. This new sales team would be required to sell products through outbound telemarketing. This group of women, all in their fifties, with over 20 years of work experience taking orders on the telephone, were so frantic by the time we got to them that we had to begin with stress management training before beginning any sales training. The lesson? Skills, aptitude, and talent for the work should be considered when making changes just as if you were hiring a new employee for a position.

Next there should be incentives. Not incentives in the traditional sense, but some positive outcome that the new change brings. It is important to establish the benefits to the change to help people develop buy-in. In the example mentioned earlier, the new telemarketing team was going to keep their existing pay and have a bonus program for new accounts they could open. An incentive can also be a work benefit such as "This software will help you reduce the paperwork for each customer and save you an average of five minutes per transaction."

You also need to consider the resources needed to help your team through the change. These might be manuals, access to people support, time needed to learn the new way, or other more tangible resources that may be required to implement the change. In the example above, I convinced my client to let me work on the floor for a few days acting as the telesales manager, since no such role existed. I was able to provide support and coaching during the first few critical days of the new role.

Last but not least, a plan for action is needed. How will the new change happen? To build engagement, get the team involved in this step in order to secure greater commitment to the change. Without a plan, people will be spinning their wheels while trying to adjust to the change. In my example, I worked out phone scripts for my client with contingencies so the team had a plan to follow regardless of the direction a call would take. Not that I wanted them to read scripts, but to help them feel completely prepared and to be successful in this new role. We adjusted these with the team's input as we got some real call experience and the team felt far more confident in the ability to be successful in the new role.

Action: Analyze the last big change you rolled out. How was it received? What aspects of the model above were present? What could you have provided to help your team accept the change more readily? How can you use this in the next change you bring to your team?

35 He Who Has the Gold, Rules

She has told me a number of times that when someone makes an error, "they treat you like bad kids at school."

Just kidding. Rule 35 is really the "other" golden rule: do unto others, as you would have them do unto you. Before beginning the actual writing for this book, I did some informal research on LinkedIn and asked the question "If you could name just one rule every manager should know, what would it be?" In just 2 days, I had 137 responses and I shut down the question before it got out of hand. I reviewed a variety of unique answers, but there was one answer that was repeated again and again: the golden rule.

I could not help but wonder why so many would suggest it? Was it because all my respondents had managers who embraced the golden rule, and this had made a big impression on them? Or could it be just the opposite: they had managers who they wished had followed this rule? We will never know for sure of course.

I think that at the core all humans want to be treated with respect. My daughter, Sarah, was working two jobs over the summer and learning lots about the world of work as she made plans for her future. It has been interesting to hear her contrast the two organizations, both of which hire lots of teenagers. She was returning to the first organization after working there last summer. She took the second job because she found it paid more, but could not give up last year's job because she enjoyed it so much.

Since almost the first day of job number two, she has commented on her concern about the management style of the organization. She has told me a number of times that when someone makes an error, "they treat you like bad kids at school." Her most recent story involved a new employee who arrived late on his first day on the job. He was quite upset saying the paper he was given at hiring had hours on it that were inconsistent with the posted schedule for that day. On the next day he went to work, the same thing happened again, and the young man was even more frustrated and seemed embarrassed. But the manager jumped all over him, in front of all the other employees. Sarah later told the manager that she felt that the employee was sincere and that he deserved a bit more trust. Her boss advised her that if she had worked as a manager for as long as he had, she would know how people lie to make their behavior appear innocent when really they are just lazy and irresponsible. I could tell that extra bit of money was losing its luster quickly and that she would probably not work for this organization again next summer.

Everyone wants the same basic treatment from his or her manager: fairness, courtesy, respect, trust, and the opportunity to succeed. These are the things the golden rule instructs us to do and, if followed, they build goodwill and engagement in the team. Use the golden rule as an overall guide; it covers a lot when it comes to management.

Action: How do you want to be treated? Make a list. Then for fun, ask each team member to make a list of how he or she wants to be treated. Behaviorally we are all different, so these needs may vary a bit from person to person in how they are expressed. At a team meeting, have each person share his personal needs and tell the team how well each item has been satisfied. Talk about the needs that are currently not being met by the team. Discuss how the team can meet these needs.

36 Build Acceptance, Reject Prejudices

The truth is, you cannot be secretive when it comes to hate.

It is shocking when we are suddenly confronted with overt acts of prejudice and when a new horrible hate crime hits the news, but what about the more subtle varieties of this problem that occur every day in the workplace? They may not hit the news and may seem obscure or, as I said earlier, subtle, but not to the people targeted by them. I'll never forget the words a participant shared in a Middle Eastern Religion course I was taking as we discussed racial profiling. He told us that there was not a day in his life that someone did not remind him that he was black. How very sad for all of us that we continue to act this way.

Many managers turn a blind eye to these issues wanting to believe that these concerns are all cleaned up and neatly tucked away in the past. Yet, just miles from where I live and work, we've had open displays of racism with confederate flags being displayed and garbage being thrown at black students in one of our local high schools. Last week, a client shared that an e-mail had been found circulating in her organization with jokes about people with disabilities. While this is bad enough, the organization actually serves people with disabilities. Another major employer in our community was in the news when e-mails with racial slurs were circulated. These events are not unique to my own little community—they are happening in your workplace too.

So what is all this talk of tolerance we hear about in the workplace? To me, it seems that having "tolerance" as a goal is terribly misguided. It is sort of like saying, "Okay, I will tolerate you at work, but just so you know, I really despise people like you and I am not about to change." Tolerance is not a team approach, or the way to build engagement on your team. What you really need as a goal is acceptance. Acceptance says: "I accept that we are different; I accept we may have different values, different beliefs, different heritage, or different characteristics; but the world is big enough to hold our differences and we can both be enriched through the uniqueness we each bring to this team."

Sadly, it seems that for many, feelings of intolerance really are just below the surface ready to come out when some unknown incident triggers them. In fact, according to a recent poll by the Washington Post and ABC News,[39] nearly half of all Americans say race relations in the country are in bad shape, and three in ten acknowledge feelings of racial prejudice.

There is no place for prejudice of any kind in your team. No gender related, sexual preference related, racial, age, or religiously motivated prejudices for your team. Besides killing engagement, these are forms of hatred and are just wrong.

The truth is, you cannot be secretive when it comes to hate. It comes out because it is central to who you are. Author Bob Conklin[40] once said: "You cannot, not communicate." What beliefs are being communicated in your team? Have you taken time to examine and act on these beliefs lately?

Action: Communication and opportunities for your team to connect can go a very long way in helping people to discover their common humanity. Sometimes teams need to tap into the resources and professionals who are skilled in helping teams work through more serious issues. If you feel your team needs more formal support, don't delay. Seek the help you need and monitor these issues regularly to check the progress toward the goal of acceptance.

37 Honesty Is Always the Best Policy

Should any of us be surprised to learn that people do not like being deceived?

We arrived for our vacation in the Pocono Mountains in time to enjoy a perfect Pennsylvania autumn. We could only spare 3 days away from work, and I was eagerly anticipating our annual hike on the Appalachian Trail. As we checked in, we discovered our timeshare had been purchased by a new entity who invited us to a short meeting to "solicit our feedback as owners." I didn't want to go, but Rick suggested we should, since we'd been owners for many years.

We arrived at the appointed time the next morning and quickly realized that we had been completely misled about the purpose of the meeting. In fact, it was not a meeting at all, but rather a sales presentation with a seasoned arm-wrestling veteran, trained in all the latest manipulative sales techniques. He told us we had somehow missed out on a once-in-a-lifetime offer to transfer our three timeshare weeks into some new metric used to get higher trade value. Perhaps we had ignored a mailing they had sent to us earlier in the year. Then, later, as we were trying to end the meeting, he sprung a "deal" on us that was in conflict with what he had told us earlier. As we tried to leave, he asked us to give his supervisor feedback on his performance, and we found this was just another trick to have the "supervisor" put yet another "deal" in front of us. As we finally managed to exit the building we were astonished to be handed $50 cash for having sat through all the abuse we'd endured. We were confused and dumbfounded by the entire experience.

On the first day back to work following our little vacation, our phone rang and the person on the other end wanted to confirm our printer model number, saying he was from our copier supply company. When I asked him to repeat where he was calling from he promptly hung up on me. Then, a few days later, I had a call from someone claiming to be from our telephone provider, wanting to save us money on the business package on our phone lines. When our next bill arrived I discovered I had unknowingly authorized a change of our service providers. I had been fooled again!

Just to be sure, I've asked a few people to check that I was not wearing a big sign on my back that says, "believes everything you tell her" ... but sure enough, I am clean. Should any of us be surprised to learn that people do not like being deceived? Yet, some businesses use deception as a strategy, and managers and team leaders teach employees how to use deceitful techniques to win business. I do not feel that these approaches can be successful long-term strategies, even if a few people (like me) are gullible enough to fall for them once (okay, every time).

According to Yaankelovich Partners,[41] a marketing services consultancy, 80% of consumers think American businesses are too concerned about making a profit and not concerned enough about their responsibilities to workers, consumers, and the environment. I wonder if employees can really be engaged in organizations that ask, and expect, them to be dishonest. I feel that most of us have an inner need to be truthful. By asking team members to be dishonest you are immediately putting them at odds with the job. How can this climate create engagement, success, or any positive outcome?

Action: Make it your policy to be truthful and to employ only marketing and selling methods that are truthful. Should you discover gross deception as a strategy in your organization's marketing mix, call the organization to task. Discuss your sales and service approach with your team to be sure there are no practices that could mislead customers.

38 Give It Your All

Management itself is a profession. For some it is truly an art form. For others it is the part of the job that is most dreaded.

Not long after joining my husband Rick at The TEAM Approach[42] we were working on a project with a pharmaceutical firm. There was a large team of trainers on the project and at the end of each day, we would have a debriefing session sharing ideas and techniques that seemed to get good results. On my very first day on the project, I wrapped up at the appointed time. As I left my classroom I went immediately to Rick's room to join him in making the trek to the appointed meeting place. Upon arriving in his classroom, however, I found him still busily working with a number of folks from his class, assisting them one-on-one, answering their questions, and providing personal support. As I observed him in action, I remember thinking to myself that the scheduled day was finished, why didn't he wrap it up and "get out of there."

Afterward, I thought about this incident a number of times and something about my own behavior that evening was very troubling to me. I realized that for some reason I was not fully engaged in the process, I was merely going through the motions of getting information into the hands of my class and leaving them to their own devices to work out the subtleties of it all. But not Rick. He was hard at it, making sure every last person got what they needed before he was satisfied that it was time to close up his shop. As I thought about it some more, I felt certain that his class was more responsive to the material; they were more engaged learners, because of his own engagement and commitment to give it his all.

Rick was role modeling his commitment to personal excellence that day and in doing so he was challenging me, without even knowing it, to examine my own commitment to such. As I did, I found it wanting, and I had to do some real soul-searching for a period of time to determine if this chosen profession was really what I wanted. I had to work through "my own stuff" and, after examining all my personal fears and shortcomings along with my strengths and gifts, I decided that this profession was the way I would choose to live my life. Now this is important, so I hope you are paying attention. I said, I decided that this was how I would choose to offer my talents to the world. It wasn't some job I applied for and got, it was a choice based on an assessment of my strengths (and limitations) that this was the right career for me and I wanted to give it all I had to offer.

Management itself is a profession. For some it is truly an art form. For others it is the part of the job that is most dreaded. If you find yourself in this second category, I encourage you to do your own soul-searching around this critical role you play in your organization. It is far too important to live in conflict with it. Your role is key to the engagement of your team. If you focus mostly on the task component of your job and pay attention to the team only in times of crisis, you are missing out on numerous opportunities to increase engagement just through your simple interest and involvement. The old expression "it's not rocket science" holds true for engagement. It's created with plain, simple interest in the team. An investment of you makes the difference. Try it and watch the result.

Action: Reflect on how you can give more to your role of manager. How can you offer more of yourself and your special talents to your team? Pick something and get started.

39

Know What You Want

In each of these cases, I would discover the most amazing coincidence: these managers had teams who did not deliver.

My husband and I raised three children without television to avoid its negative influence on the life of our family. Instead, we developed a personal library of classic films and visited the public library often to borrow books and good films for our family to enjoy. An interesting, yet unanticipated, consequence of this decision was our family's lack of exposure to advertising through commercial TV. We often noticed this at gatherings where discussions of the latest new miracle product took place which we had somehow managed to live without. It was at a family Christmas party, however, that we realized the biggest benefit of our decision. When our daughter climbed onto Santa's lap, and was asked what she wanted for Christmas, she responded very honestly with "What have you got?" We never had a meltdown shopping experience or child who would badger us for weeks on end until they could have the latest and greatest "whatever." Our children, for the most part, grew up "want free!"

Success in life, however, truly does come from knowing what we want, but this knowing does not come from outside influences. It comes from within. "Ask and you shall receive" are powerful words that speak an important truth about what life delivers: we must know what we want before we can find it. This is so true in the workplace, and particularly for those of us in leadership roles. How often I have heard supervisors and managers in workshops discuss somewhat negative views of their teams. They seemed to anticipate a lack of results. And guess what? In each of these cases I would discover the most amazing coincidence: these managers had teams who did not deliver.

It is wonderful when you discover a group of leaders who know what they want and set out to build it from the beginning. Such is the case with a team of partners who built a small company called Reprint Management Services (RMS). This team of partners had all previously worked in the printing industry, but they had been subjected to a management style that did not value its employees or encourage a team approach. When the RMS partners hired their first employee, they made a conscious decision to build an organization that would embrace a team approach. Their success had kept them in the top ten places to work in the State of Pennsylvania ever since the beginning of the "best places to work" contest began there.[43] They recently sold RMS and are now building a new company called Nxtbook Media, Inc.,[44] using the same principles of teamwork, positive expectations, valuing creativity, and fun.

Touring either company under this inspired leadership team is a treat one never forgets. Each organization is comprised of teams that have their own identities and unique personalities. The teams gently compete, and the work environment is designed to facilitate team interaction and mutual support. Each member of the company is valued and individual success is celebrated in creative ways. For example, an intercom announcement might broadcast sales made by someone providing immediate recognition. Or, everyone might be summoned to a wacky spontaneous gathering in the lobby to watch someone read the note accompanying the arrival of flowers they received on a special occasion. The partners knew they wanted a new kind of company that valued teamwork and fun. They also knew they wanted to be successful. They have achieved both of these goals in big ways!

Action: Engagement begins with wanting it, envisioning it. So, what about you and your team? Are you happy with what you see before you? Are you clear about what you want? You begin by having absolute clarity around what you want to build—you must know what it is that you want. Get together with your team and review your organization's mission, then work together to build a team mission that supports it.

40 Engaged Teams Get the facts

How often had I missed the opportunity to get all the facts and left with a completely wrong perception of how things went?

Arriving for a recent appointment, I was asked to sit outside a conference room where a meeting with a potential vendor was winding down. I was able to hear the vendor closing the meeting, explaining why her firm was the best choice and suggesting next steps. I listened to her friendly departure, affirming everyone as she left. Before I was invited in, the team quickly debriefed the meeting that just concluded. Their impression of how things went was not nearly as optimistic as I had expected. They agreed on two issues that seemed to be a showstopper for this vendor.

Wow! As I sat there, I began to feel queasy. How often had I missed the opportunity to get all the facts and left with a completely wrong perception of how things went? How often had I missed key concerns and opportunities to build trust and clarify information? While this example comes from a selling perspective, it has huge implications for anyone desiring to create an engaged work team.

As a manager, you are constantly "selling" to your team. Every time you position a new project and want commitment and creative mindshare or have a great idea, you are attempting to influence and sell your team. Has a project or idea of yours ever stalled before getting a serious chance to realize its potential? When facilitating an innovation process we support team buy-in and engagement by helping team members identify and use their natural team talents.

Some members of the team are more likely to have a natural talent for generating ideas, but they may have little interest in building these sketchy ideas into a fleshed out plan of action. They are easy to identify as they love brainstorming and creative thinking. In fact, they may actually feel that the process is complete once they have offered their original, great ideas. Beginning an innovation process with an ideation session that focuses exclusively on brainstorming and creative thinking will engage those who have a strong natural talent for ideation.

Once the ideation process is complete, we facilitate a handoff to team members who have a natural talent for identifying the very best ideas from the list and building substance around those ideas. These folks are talented at building a plan and selling it to decision makers.

But before the process goes any further, it is important to get the facts, lest the team end up like our friend the vendor—left out in the cold. To get the facts, the team needs to draw upon the talent of those members who instinctively enjoy playing devil's advocate and are naturally talented at finding the problems or shortfalls in the plan. As any new challenges or errors are uncovered, the ideation process begins again, this time to generate ideas that will address these new discoveries. This cycle is repeated until such time that everyone agrees the plan is ready to implement. When the team gets to this point, it is time for a handoff to the team members who have talent for developing delivery systems that will bring this plan into reality.

By tapping into each team member's talent in the process, concerns and pitfalls can be fully explored, which may create problems down the road. No surprises should pop up causing some members not to support the end result, because all have been involved at the stage of the process that matches their greatest strength. The facts are not ignored or feared, but offered as a tool that helps the team produce the highest quality outcome.

Action: Observe and identify team members with each of these talents. Then try this process with your team as you solve a problem or implement a new change. Highlight each stage for the team as you progress through the process.

41

Ask, Don't Tell

He then asked an important question: "How do you think this situation is impacting our other customers out there?"

One summer while in college, I worked at a pizza shop in Rehobeth Beach, Delaware. This place was so busy that the owner had a small apartment attached to the shop for quick naps when his workday extended beyond his regular 16-hour shift. In the heat of summer, with a dozen or more ovens going, customers would be waiting around the block to get a table. The owner functioned as the manager of a team of mostly teenagers; and he did it with amazing patience and grace.

I learned a number of important lessons while working on this job, but the most significant involved a pitcher of beer. During dinner rush one Friday, two women seated in my station appeared to have had some alcohol before arriving. They ordered a pizza and a pitcher of Michelob®,[45] our top-shelf and most expensive beer. They began enjoying their beer while waiting for their pie. Just before polishing off their pitcher, they summoned me to their table to complain they'd been served Budweiser[46] instead of Michelob® and demanded a free pitcher for their trouble. Having personally observed their beer being poured, I decided they had some integrity issues so I wasn't feeling helpful, nor responding cooperatively.

As their voices grew louder, I was suddenly summoned to see "the boss." He looked at me calmly from behind his desk and said, "Susan, tell me what happened out there?" After relating the story from my perspective, he asked, "What did you do?" I told him that I had refused on the basis of having personally observed the pitcher being filled. He paused as if he were thinking about the situation, which gave me time to think more about it too. Then he asked: "How much do you think a pitcher of beer costs me?" I paused, not being sure, and he shared that it was less than fifty cents. Then he pointed to the television monitor where we could both observe the dining room and hear the loud unfriendly remarks still spewing from the mouths of my two guests. He then asked an important question: "How do you think this situation is impacting our other customers out there?" This question rattled me as I thought about the situation more closely and considered the impact it would have on my tips. Finally, he asked a question that still amazes me today: "What do you think you should do now?" Well, I did not even hesitate. I said I would gladly provide a free pitcher of beer and apologize to get things back to normal for the other customers as quickly as possible.

Just by asking me these questions, it seemed he had invited me to act on his behalf and everything seemed a little different as I returned to my station. I felt empowered to use my best judgment based on what seemed right for the business. I felt I was trusted and respected; and I was only a kid! This manager understood the art of using questions as a learning and engagement tool. Using this approach, he could determine my reasoning and problem-solving capabilities, and adjust his responses accordingly. By utilizing a questioning approach, instead of a telling approach, you can help your team become more skilled and more committed. Now that's engagement!

Action: Make a list of all the teachable moments that have occurred in the last few weeks and reflect on how you approached each one. Did you ask, or did you tell, as you attempted to coach the team member? What personal barriers might you experience in using an asking style and how might you overcome these?

42

These Are My Rules, What Are Yours?

Did you ever have a a coloring book when you were young? Do you remember how you began with a blank book and you filled in the "content" based on your unique interpretation. Consider rule 42 to be your personal employee engagement coloring book. I'd like to challenge you to fill in those rules that have been left out. Surely there must be hundreds of rules of employee engagement. Here is a short list of rules I've run out of room for:

Be visible
Be responsive
Lighten it up
Inspire innovation
Celebrate success
Be flexible
Be on time
Throw a lifeline
Keep your promises
Mistakes are learning tools
Try another way
Focus on behavior
Breathe
Get a life
Your employees have a life
Build a team
Challenge conventional thinking

Perhaps you'd like to write about one of these rules, or suggest a rule of your own? Why not share your rules so others can have the benefit of your insight and experience? I'd like to invite you to bring your rules, stories, and experiences to a special blog created for just this purpose. Join me there and add your thoughts to this important conversation. Visit the *42 Rules of Employee Engagement* blog at: http://www.42rules.com/employeeengagement_blog/

I will look forward to meeting you there and to having your assistance in coloring in more of this picture. All the best,

Susan Stamm
susan@teamapproach.com

Recommended Employee Engagement Books

***Closing the Engagement Gap* by Julie Gebauer and Don Lowman**
Effective leaders understand that the most valuable source of competitive advantage is a workforce that consistently and willingly performs its best. But that happens only when people are engaged in their work. So how do you, as a leader, manager, or individual employee, help create engagement? How do you close the gap for yourself and others between doing what's required and going the distance? Gebauer and Lowman share Towers Perrin's ground-breaking research, as well as knowledge they've built helping companies tap employee potential and improve business results. In addition, they draw on a rich vein of anecdotes from CEOs, managers, and employees at eight extraordinary organizations. Download a Bookends Bookclub podcast interview with Julie Gebauer discussing this book: http://www.bookendsbookclub.net.
To purchase this book visit: http://www.towersperrin.com/gap/buy.htm

***Fired Up or Burned Out* by Michael Lee Stallard, Carolyn Dewing-Hommes, and Jason Pankau**
A company who has employees who show up and do their job and go home is nowhere near as effective as a company whose employees are connected to each other. Employee disengagement is a widespread malady in American organizations, causing the loss of billions of dollars, hours of dissatisfaction, and work lives lacking true value. This book points that way to the three key actions necessary to transform even a lethargic, disconnected organization

or office into an impassioned, innovative, and thriving workplace. Download a Bookends Bookclub podcast interview with Michael Lee Stallard discussing this book: http://www.bookendsbookclub.net. To purchase this book or learn more visit: http://www.fireduporburnedout.com/

Contented Cows Moove Faster by Richard Hadden

Workplace studies have repeatedly shown that most people, by their own admission, could contribute significantly more effort to their jobs if they really wanted to. Residing within each of us is a reservoir of effort that remains entirely under our personal control ... discretionary effort. It dwells in the gap between what's required of us and what we're actually capable of. We call it *Oomph!* Good leaders at every level strive daily to get the benefit of that extra effort. *Contented Cows Moove Faster* is about how they do it, and how you can do it. It's about real people with real jobs going the extra mile, and the leadership behaviors that cause them to want to do it. To purchase this book or learn more visit: http://www.contentedcows.com/buy_the_book.html

Engaging the Hearts and Minds of All Your Employees by Lee Colan

Learn "how to" for inspiring your team so they deliver unparalleled value to your customers. Proven at Fortune 500 companies across the globe, Colan's simple but powerful formula is this: if you meet your employees' basic intellectual and emotional needs, they will perform at peak ability. They will be energetic and innovative, and they will keep your customers satisfied and loyal. To do this, he equips you with the practical tools to engage employees at all levels, and ignite the fire of "Passionate Performance." Packed with proven strategies for meeting your people's needs as well as instructive examples from stellar companies, including Nordstrom, Southwest Airlines, Toyota, and General Electric, *Engaging the Hearts and Minds of All Your Employees* is your field guide for conquering your competition ... one employee at a time. Download a Bookends Bookclub podcast interview with Lee Colan discussing this book: http://www.bookendsbookclub.net. To purchase this book visit: http://www.thelgroup.com/p_Engage/engage.asp

Engaged Leadership: Building a Culture to Overcome Employee Disengagement by Clint Swindall

In good times, employee engagement is needed to help an organization thrive. In bad times, employee engagement is *required* to help an organization survive. Professional speaker and author Clint Swindall shows leaders at all levels how to enhance employee engagement in his book *Engaged Leadership: Building a Culture to Overcome Employee Disengagement* (John Wiley & Sons, 2007). Readers will learn how to build that culture by breaking down the art of effective leadership into three primary areas that all leaders must master in order to inspire and engage their employees: directional leadership, which build a consensus for the vision; motivational leadership, which inspires people to pursue the vision; and organizational leadership, which develops the team to realize the vision. To learn more, visit www.verbalocity.com, or get your copy today at www.amazon.com.

I Quit, but Forgot to Tell You by **Terri Kabachnick**
Disengagement statistics are telling, but they don't convey the entire story. You must look at the human issues behind the numbers. That's why much of *I Quit but Forgot to Tell You* is premised on Terri's real-life experiences—first as a professional in the field of retail, then as a retail strategist and advisor. The ideas and recommendations, however, are equally suited for all industries; they are straightforward, logical truths that utilize the logic of human nature to achieve the goals of both the individual and the organization. To purchase this book or for more information visit: http://www.kabachnick.com/

The Essential Guide to Employee Engagement by **Sarah Cook**
Businesses have long recognized the importance of cultivating proud, motivated, and loyal employees. In fact, organizations that still operate with the mentality that workers should do their jobs and keep their mouths shut are likely to flounder. These days, the old style of management has largely disappeared, but so has the trust that once existed between employer and employee. Job seekers no longer expect to find lifetime positions within one company. Layoffs and cutbacks in a difficult economic environment have generated fear and suspicion among employees. Companies recognize that their long-term viability depends on finding, retaining, and motivating good employees. Sarah Cook competently explains why every organization should make employee engagement a priority and provides numerous examples of British and American companies that embrace and benefit from employee engagement. To purchase this book visit: www.amazon.com

The New Rules of Engagement by **Mike Johnson**
This book offers practical, down-to-earth solutions, providing firsthand insights into engaging today's employee. How many employees care enough about their work or your organization to do anything other than the bare minimum? How many would stay if they got another job offer? Why should YOU care? Well, highly engaged employees are six times less likely to be planning to leave their jobs than those who are disengaged. Mike Johnson argues that there are simple, direct ways to develop a NEW psychological contract between employer and employee. And you can start writing that new contract by recognizing that the talk of work–life balance is the wrong way round as far as your employees are concerned—they are much more interested in their LIFE–WORK balance. Successful employers today know that life comes before work. To purchase this book visit: http://www.mikeajohnson.com/publication.html

Employee Engagement: The People First Approach to Building a Business by David Croston

Croston's book contains a succinct overview of the subject, a roadmap to guide the first-time traveler, a series of interviews with executives who have enjoyed success in this area, and a large number of helpful hints and tips. To purchase this book visit: http://www.amazon.com/

Follow this Path by Curt Coffman

What do the greatest organizations in the world have in common? They know their most valuable resource is human—their employees and their customers. And the best companies understand two important facts: people are emotional first and rational second, and because of that, employees and customers must be emotionally engaged in order for the organization to reach its full potential. To purchase this book visit: http://www.amazon.com

Engagement Is Not Enough by Keith Ayers

Lack of employee engagement is like a cancer eating away at your organization's vital organs. It saps your organization's strength directly affecting your organization's ability to achieve customer satisfaction, productivity, and profitability that you know you could achieve. Ayers presents a compelling argument that the focus on engagement has failed because leaders thing engagement can be bought through bonuses, benefits, and share options. That is like trying to cure cancer with aspirin or band-aids. The cure of disengagement is for leaders to look into the mirror at the leadership they provide. In this in-depth explanation to get every employee to want to perform at their best, Ayers challenges leaders to stop focusing on engagement and to ignite the fire of passion in their employees. Download a Bookends Bookclub podcast interview with Keith Ayers discussing this book: http://www.bookendsbookclub.net. To purchase this book visit: http://www.engagementisnotenough.com/

Community: The Structure of Belonging by Peter Block

"My intent," Block writes, "is to provide structural ways to create the experience of belonging, not just in those places where people come to just be together socially, but especially in places where we least expect it. This includes those places where people come together to get something done. These are our meetings, dialogues, conferences, planning processes—all those occasions where we gather to reflect on and decide the kind of future we want for ourselves." This book is written to support those who care for the well-being of their communities. It is for anyone who wants to be part of an organization, neighborhood, city, or country that works for all, and who have the faith and the energy to create such a place. Download a Bookends Bookclub podcast interview with Peter Block discussing this book: http://www.bookendsbookclub.net. To purchase this book or for more information visit: http://www.designedlearning.com/

Lead Well and Prosper by Nick McCormick

A straightforward guide for managers at all levels. Each chapter begins with a humorous but unfortunately all-too-true scenario—complete with a cast of characters and illustrations—demonstrating the common mistakes managers make. Then recommended tips are included to help overcome the problem. A list of dos and don'ts—which cut right to the chase—follows. Actions that can be taken immediately to implement the strategy are listed at the end of each section. Appendices list the dos and don'ts in one place for easy reference, and include a quiz that determines a manager's effectiveness. Download a Bookends Bookclub podcast interview with Nick McCormick discussing this book: http://www.bookendsbookclub.net. To purchase this book visit: http://www.begoodventures.com/products.html

Ready Set Engage by Stephanie Oden

Meet Harvey, a 20-year employee and executive at Precision Industries. Harvey is reeling from the resignation of one of his key employees, the lackluster performance of another, and the possibility of losing his largest customer. Fortunately, he meets Kathryn who introduces him to the Ready, Set, Engage (RSE) path. Before long, Harvey is actively engaged in developing an energized staff committed to creating lasting customer relationships. Along the RSE path, Harvey also forms stronger connections with the important people in his life. This book is a must-have for today's leaders who are pursuing personal excellence, innovative teams, and excited customers. To purchase this book visit: http://www.livewireconsultinggroup.com/

The Three Signs of a Miserable Job by Pat Lencioni

Managers and employees are presented with a revolutionary yet simple model for making any job more rewarding and fulfilling. To purchase this book visit: http://www.amazon.com/

Innovation On Demand by Allen Fahden

This books discuss the roles that are needed for a team to innovate, solve problems and move work forward. The key to engagement is to enable people offer their greatest talents to the work process- this keeps them satisfied and feeling they are making their best contribution to the team. This book offers a hand-off process that prevents natural conflict which can occur between the different strengths found on the team. To purchase this book visit: http://www.teamapproach.com

Intrinsic Motivation at Work by Kenneth W. Thomas

In today's organizations, employee engagement is vital- more is required of workers than ever before. In this new edition of his classic book, Thomas draws on the latest research findings to identify the key to employee engagement: intrinsic motivation. Only intrinsic rewards- rewards that come directly from the work itself- encourage the profound commitment and sense of ownership needed for a truly engaged workforce. Thomas identifies four intrinsic rewards, explains exactly how and why they build engagement, and provides a diagnostic framework to evaluate which need boosting and how to boost them. To order this book: http://www.bkconnection.com/

Real Time Strategic Change: How to Involve an Entire Organization in Fast and Far Reaching Change by Robert W Jacobs

The most successful organizations will be those that are capable of rapidly and effectively bringing about fundamental, lasting, system-wide changes. This book offers a redesign of the way organizations change and provides a practical, hands-on, step by step roadmap through the entire change process. Interactive large group meetings form the foundation of this approach, enabling hundreds and even thousands of people to collaborate in creating their collective future. Change happens faster because the total organization is the "in group" that decides which changes are needed; and the actions people take on a daily basis are aligned behind the overall strategic direction they helped to create. Download a Bookends Bookclub podcast interview with Robert W Jacobs discussing this book: http://www.bookendsbookclub.net. To purchase this book: http://www.windsofchangegroup.com/

First Break All The Rules by Marcus Buckingham and Curt Coffman

Buckingham and Coffman present the remarkable findings of their massive in-depth study of great managers across a variety of situations. Companies need to find and keep the very best employees using pay, benefits, promotions and training, but these well intentioned efforts often miss the mark. The front line manager is the key to attracting and retaining the best talent. Buckingham and Coffman explain how the best managers select an employee for talent rather than skills or experience; how they set expectations for him or her-they define the right outcomes rather than the right steps; how they motivate people- they build on each person's strength rather than trying to fix his weakness; and finally, how great managers develop people- they find the right fit for each person- not the next rung on the ladder. To order this book: http://www.amazon.com

Employee Engagement Resources

The Power of Appreciative Inquiry by Diana Whitney and Amanda Trosten-Bloom

The Power of Appreciative Inquiry describes a wildly popular new approach to organizational change that dramatically improves performance by encouraging people to study, discuss, learn from, and build on what's working, rather than simply trying to fix what's not. The authors illustrate each step in the AI process using actual events at Hunter Douglas. Download a Bookends Bookclub podcast interview with Diana Whitney discussing this book: http://www.bookendsbookclub.net. To purchase this book visit: http://www.amazon.com

The World Cafe by Juanita Brown with David Isaacs

The World Cafe is a flexible, easy-to-use process for fostering collaborative dialogue, sharing mutual knowledge, and discovering new opportunities for action. Based on living systems thinking, this innovative approach creates dynamic networks of conversation that can catalyze an organization or community's own collective intelligence around its most important questions. Gain practical tips for hosting "conversations that matter" in groups of any size, strengthening both personal relationships and people's capacity to shape the future together. Download a Bookends Bookclub podcast interview with David Isaacs discussing this book: http://www.bookendsbookclub.net. To purchase this book visit: http://www.theworldcafe.com/

The Employee Engagement Network
Join a community dedicated to engagement. The Employee Engagement Network was started by David Zinger and created on Ning. The network is a collection of over 1000 members interested in employee engagement. Members meet and discuss in groups, forums, chats, and blogs. A great place to connect for discussion on EE topics, books and more. Membership is free. To join today visit: http://employeeengagement.ning.com/

How to Engage People When You Don't Have Time by Dick Axelrod
Everyone knows that employee engagement is important. Engaged people are more productive, have less absenteeism, and provide better customer service compared to their disengaged counterparts. But many organizations pursue strategies through complicated programs that take years to implement. Engagement doesn't take years—it can occur in minutes. Download a Bookends Bookclub podcast interview with Dick Axelrod discussing this engagement tool: http://www.bookendsbookclub.net.
To purchase this program or learn more visit:
http://everydayengagement.com/

Engaging Ideas Card Pack
The Engaging ideas card pack provides practical exercises and ideas designed to help better inspire employee engagement and change to deliver higher business performance. It is not a "best-practice" guide. It is a practical toolkit—employee engagement and change inspiration "in a box." To order visit: http://www.engagingideas.co.uk/

50 Activities for Employee Engagement by Peter R. Garber
50 Activities for Employee Engagement by Peter R. Garber, author and human resource professional for nearly 30 years, is a collection of skill-building activities that will help you understand what employee engagement really means, how it can help your organization, and how to create and maintain an engaged workforce. The activities help you define employee engagement, measure the current level of engagement in your organization, overcome obstacles, motivate employees to become engaged, and even consider how world-famous leaders might lead engagement in the workplace. Each activity is presented on a different aspect of employee engagement that can be completed in 30–45 minutes. To order visit: http://www.hrdpress.com. Download a Bookends Bookclub podcast interview with Dick Axelrod discussing this engagement tool: http://www.bookendsbookclub.net

42 Rules of Engagement Toolbox

Host a *42 Rules of Employee Engagement* "Book Club" and download free "Action Templates" to track progress on the rules. Host learning circles, mentor groups, lunch and learns, or internal book discussion groups. Download templates and forms that relate to the actions that are suggested throughout the book. http://www.teamapproach.com/42rulesresources.asp

Rule 42: Add input on each rule and/or write your own rule(s) on employee engagement and post them on the *42 Rules of Employee Engagement* Blog: http://www.42rules.com/employeeengagement_blog/

Interact with Employee Engagement Authors: Join Susan Stamm as she interviews authors of employee engagement books every month on Bookends. Hear archived interviews, download podcasts, attend live sessions, read and discuss the books with the authors on Linkedin: http://www.bookendsbookclub.net

Assess Your Team in Nine Key Areas of Team Performance:

Purpose
Communication
Performance
Feedback
Role clarity
Conflict management
Problem solving
Work environment
Team time

Try our free Team Check Up: http://www.teamapproach.com/checkup.asp

Assess Leaders on Eleven Key Engagement Competencies

Leading by example
Encouraging innovation
Innovative problem solving
Decision making
Delegating
Observing
Listening
Team building
Resolving conflict
Performance coaching
Performance management

Try our free Team Leader Check Up:
http://www.teamapproach.com/TeamLeaderCheckup.asp

Gather FREE Tools and Ideas to Build your Team

1. Pit the Pairs—use this tool to make team decisions:
   http://www.teamapproach.com/42rulesresources.asp
2. Calculate the value of one customer with our customer service calculator: http://www.teamapproach.com/42rulesresources.asp
3. Get posters, activities and ideas to build you team when you sign up for The TEAM Approach® newsletter:
   http://www.teamapproach.com/mm/subscribe.asp
4. Rule 7 suggests everyone needs feedback. Use this exercise to help illustrate that in a powerful way:
   http://www.teamapproach.com/42rulesresources.asp
5. Celebrate the diversity of gifts on your team and illustrate their importance to your team with this fable:
   http://www.teamapproach.com/42rulesresources.asp
6. Rule 4 discusses the challenges we face in communicating. Try an exercise called Words, Words, Words with your team to illustrate the challenges highlighted in this chapter and discuss what the team can do to avoid the pitfalls:
   http://www.teamapproach.com/42rulesresources.asp
7. Get your team to envision a best team and then work to build one:
   http://www.teamapproach.com/42rulesresources.asp
8. Rule 41 provides a glimpse at a powerful coaching model that will build team engagement. Learn more about how critical communication is to this process at this link:
   http://www.teamapproach.com/42rulesresources.asp

1. Christina Baldwin is an author, educator, speaker, and retreat leader. She is known for her groundbreaking work in the fields of personal writing, group process, and spirituality. With author, Ann Linnea, she is cofounder of PeerSpirit, Inc., offering a wide variety of consulting seminars, practica, and wilderness programs to individuals and groups. Baldwin is the author of *One to One, Self-Understanding through Journal Writing; Life's Companion, Journal Writing as a Spiritual Quest; Calling the Circle*; and *The Seven Whispers*. http://www.peerspirit.com/index.html

2. Employee Engagement Scores relates to the data published through large-scale survey work published by various organizations. Gallup's research, for example, is often cited due to the massive size of their surveys and the variety of industry sectors included in their data. Gallup has suggested that only 29% of employees are actively engaged, 54% are not engaged, with another 17% actively disengaged. http://www.tinyurl.com/cy9ydh.[1]

3. IKEA—Furniture Retailer that originated in Sweden and now has stores throughout the world. Offers a wide range of well-designed, functional home furnishing products at prices so low that most people will be able to afford them. http://www.ikea.com/

4. AT&T is the largest US provider of both local and long-distance telephone services, and DSL Internet access. AT&T is the second largest provider of wireless service in the United States, with over 77 million wireless customers, and more than 150 million total customers. http://en.wikipedia.org/wiki/AT&T

5. *The Sound of Music* a musical released in 1965 with music by Rodgers and Hammerstein. The film was directed by Robert Wise and based on the book by Maria Von Trapp called the *The Story of the Trapp Family Singers*. In the film, Julie Andrews, who plays Maria, sings a song to teach the children how to sing. This song opens with the line: "Let's start at the very beginning, a very good place to start...." For information about the *Sound of Music* including trailers visit: http://www.imdb.com/title/tt0059742/ Julie Andrews is an award-winning English actor, singer, and author.

---

1. http://www.gallup.com/consulting/52/Employee-Engagement.aspx

Read her full biography at: http://tinyurl.com/cagjfd.[2] See Julie Andrews as Elisa Doolittle on stage at: http://www.tinyurl.com/5qw6fa.[3]

6. Onboarding Process—a process of bringing new employees into the fold and helping them feel connected to the team and secure in their ability to learn the new role.

7. Pull Nurse—a term used in healthcare facilities for a nurse who is not assigned to a specific area but "pulled" to locations where staff may be short or extra staffing is needed. This role can also be called the Pool Nurse because this person is in the "nursing pool," or "float pool."

8. As reported in *USA Today*, March 2, 2007 http://www.tinyurl.com/rkzj7.[4]

9. 360 Feedback—a process for gathering feedback from multiple sources that could include one's boss, peers, direct reports, customers, vendors, and others. http://www.teamapproach.com/360feedback.asp

10. *Encyclopedia Britannica*: http://www.encyclopediacenter.com

11. *Great Books of the Western World*: http://www.tinyurl.com/dz4wcu.[5]

12. AiA Classic™ is a complete interpersonal development program that has been used worldwide over the last 50 years. It helps employees develop greater self-awareness, self-management skills, and an understanding of how their thoughts impact their personal success. Known best by its original name, Adventures in Attitudes®, the program offers 30 hours of highly experiential learning projects led by small group leaders at each table. Published today by Inscape Publishing, Inc., of Minneapolis, Minnesota, it was developed and authored by Bob Conklin and originally published by Personal Dynamics Institute. To download a white paper on AiA Classic™ visit: http://www.teamapproach.com/aiapromo.asp

13. Robert (Bob) Conklin: 1921–98 cofounder and partner of Personal Dynamics Institute; author of eight books, numerous training modules, and audio programs; and speaker. His work, especially the Adventures in Attitudes® program has touched millions worldwide. Adventures in Attitudes® and AiA Classic™ (the 50th anniversary edition of Adventures in Attitudes®) are published today by Inscape Publishing, Inc., of Minneapolis, Minnesota.

14. FaceBook—an access-free social networking site that is privately owned by Facebook, Inc. Found on the Web at http://www.facebook.com/home.php

15. Linkedin®—an access-free social networking site geared exclusively to work and professional networking. Found on the Web at http://www.linkedin.com/

16. IM—Instant Messaging: process of communicating electronically and instantly with others who are signed on to an instant messenger service such as iChat or AOL Instant Messenger.

17. *All I Really Need to Know I Learned in Kindergarten* 1986 by Robert Fulghum. Published by Ballentine Books.

18. Affirmations—a process of affirming the things you want to hold true for your life or bring into existence within your life. Affirmations are repeated to oneself silently throughout the day, read repeatedly, or proclaimed to others.

19. DISC—The book, *The Emotions of Normal People*, written by William Moulton Marston in 1928, forms the theoretical basis for the DISC model of behavior.

---

2. http://julieandrewsforum.com/biography.html
3. http://www.youtube.com/watch?v=zA7sidgFGHU
4. http://www.usatoday.com/tech/news/2006-08-30-radioshack-email-layoffs_x.htm
5. http://www.encyclopediacenter.com/great-books-western-world.html?gclid=CNG6raKf8ZgCFRHBDAod_2pA1w

Unlike Jung, Marston was not concerned with categorizing people into psychological types; rather he focussed on categorizing behavior into four types. He theorized that effective people would behave in a manner consistent with the demands and expectations of the environment. Marston published a second book on DISC, *Integrative Psychology*, in 1931. He did not develop a DISC instrument or assessment.

20. Bookends—Monthly podcast hosted by Susan Stamm, featuring author interviews. The books featured are written for leaders and HRD professionals and 2009 features books written on the topic of employee engagement. The authors provide a good tour of their books: http://www.bookendsbookclub.net. Susan also hosts a Discussion Group with the authors and anyone else who wants to join in at Linkedin®. The group is called Bookends: The Discussion: http://www.linkedin.com/

21. Tom Peter's—"Managing by Wandering Around" principle, commonly known as MBWA was popularized in the book: *In Search of Excellence* by Tom Peters and Robert Waterman 1982, Warner Books.

22. Beethoven—Ludwig van Beethoven 1770–1827 was a German composer and pianist. One of the most acclaimed composers of all time who began to go deaf in his early twenties yet continued to both compose, perform, and conduct even after going totally deaf.

23. *Immortal Beloved* is a film on the life of Beethoven with both fictitious and real elements of his life. It was released in 1995 written and directed by Bernard Rose. For more information see: http://www.imdb.com/title/tt0110116/

24. Bob Conklin—this quote appeared in the *Coordinator Magazine*, May 1986, which was published by Personal Dynamics Institute.

25. Burger King Corporation owns and franchises fast-food hamburger restaurants. Burger King Holdings has operations in the United States, Canada, Europe, the Middle East, Africa, Asia-Pacific, and Latin America. The company was founded in 1954 and is headquartered in Miami, Florida: http://www.tinyurl.com/h9m6s.[6]

26. Cicero—Roman philosopher 106 BC–43 BC. Read about Cicero on Wikipedia: http://en.wikipedia.org/wiki/Cicero

27. Quote from *As a Man Thinketh* by James Allen: http://www.tinyurl.com/9czqz.[7]

28. Blessing White—employee engagement and leadership development delivered through consulting and content, informed by ongoing research. Blessing White is a global consulting firm dedicated to creating sustainable high-performance organizations. http://www.blessingwhite.com

29. Thousand-Legger—a centipede-type insect. The name "thousand-legger" is actually a name based on illusion, an illusion born of the speed at which house centipedes move and the speed at which people tend to run from them. http://godofinsects.com/museum/display.php?sid=1690

30. SMART Goals—A process for better goal setting that enables one to know clearly if a goal has been met. The word SMART is an acronym for Specific, Measurable, Attainable, Relevant, and Time Bound. If I wanted to lose weight, for example, I would need the goal to be SPECIFIC: I want to lose 15 pounds which is a specific target. Then it needs to be MEASURABLE: I can easily measure 15 pounds by identifying my starting weight today. Next it needs to be ATTAINABLE and credible weight loss organizations suggest a pound per

---

6. http://www.bk.com/#menu=1,-1,-1
7. http://jamesallen.wwwhubs.com/think.htm

week is both achievable and safe. It also needs to be RELEVANT and since my clothing hurts and I refuse to move up a size, it is surely a relevant goal. Finally, it needs to be TIME BOUND and by looking at my calendar and choosing a date 15 weeks from today, I have a point in future in which I can assess if my SMART goal has been achieved.

31. EAP—Employee Assistance Program is a service, plan, or set of benefits that are designed for personal or family problems, including mental health, substance abuse, gambling addiction, marital problems, parenting problems, emotional problems, or financial pressures. http://tinyurl.com/dkg32v.[8]

32. Dsylexia—a learning disability that causes difficulty in learning to read. http://en.wikipedia.org/wiki/Dyslexia

33. Steve Pavlina as quoted in the *New York Times* citing workplace statistics. To see the full article visit: http://www.tinyurl.com/chzgj3.[9] For Steve's Web site visit: www.stevepavlina.com

34. *One Minute Manager* was written by Ken Blanchard, Ph.D., and Spencer Johnson, M.D., in 1981 and was published by William Marrow and Company, Inc. It is a timeless classic filled with wisdom. This fun, yet insightful book, looks at key disciplines that lead to successful people management. It shows managers how little time is needed to use these important management tools. Visit the Ken Blanchard Companies Web site: http://tinyurl.com/d5g6ol.[10]

35. Hawthorn Studies—a series of famous studies that suggested just by observing (expressing interest) a work team, their performance improves. Read all about these studies on Wikipedia: http://www.tinyurl.com/42wpx.[11]

36. Positive Leadership by Kim Cameron 2008 Berrett–Koehler Publishers. Kim Cameron is Professor of Management and Organizations at Michigan's Stephen M. Ross School of Business and Professor of Higher Education in the School of Education at the University of Michigan. He is coauthor or coeditor of ten books, including *Developing Management Skills and Positive Organizational Scholarship*, and is cofounder of the Ross School of Business Center for Positive Organizational Scholarship, which the Harvard Business Review recognized as one of the Breakthrough Ideas for 2004. *Positive Leadership* shows how to reach beyond ordinary success to achieve extraordinary effectiveness, spectacular results, and what Kim Cameron calls "positively deviant performance"—performance far above the norm.

37. Where there is not vision, the people perish. Proverbs 29:18

38. NASA story—A "story" has circulated for decades about a visit that President John Kennedy made to NASA. According to the story, while there, Kennedy asked a janitor: "What's your job?" To which came the reply: "I am putting a man on the moon." The story is a good illustration the power of alignment within organizations. When a mission is championed by an organization, employees get greater meaning from their work. If employees understand how their work contributes to these goals, greater levels of commitment and engagement are experienced. Urban legend? Perhaps, but I hope not. If you have the citation for this story, place contact me at: susan@teamapproach.com. Here are a few places this story can be found today: http://www.superjob4u.com/tag/management/

---

8. http://en.wikipedia.org/wiki/Employee_assistance_programs
9. http://www.nytimes.com/2007/05/31/fashion/31work.html
10. http://www.kenblanchard.com/
11. http://en.wikipedia.org/wiki/Hawthorne_effect

http://jeffreybjordan.blogspot.com/2006_04_01_archive.html
http://tinyurl.com/cqsrzu.[12]
39. *Washington Post* and NBC News Poll reports on race relations in June 2008 http://www.tinyurl.com/dh9v43.[13]
40. Bob Conklin quote—"You cannot, not communicate." This quote is found on the audiotaped messages that are part of the AiA Classic™ program, formally known as the Adventures in Attitudes® program. Both AiA Classic™ and Adventures in Attitudes® are published by Inscape Publishing, Inc.
41. Yaankelovich Partners—a marketing services company reports growing distrust of American business: http://www.tinyurl.com/dz4855.[14]
42. The TEAM Approach® is a team development firm dedicated to building enduring relationships and key leadership skills that drive teamwork and engagement: http://www.teamapproach.com/
43. Best places to work in Pennsylvania: http://www.tinyurl.com/d2ol7a.[15]
44. Nxtbook Media, LLC—Based in Lancaster, Pennsylvania, Nxtbook transforms the way people read on the Internet. Working with magazine publishers, catalog publishers, and corporate marketers, Nxtbook finds ways to leverage traditional print material for optimized use online: http://nxtbookmedia.com/
45. Michelob® is wholly owned and brewed by the Michelob Brewing Company.
46. Budweiser is owned and brewed by Anheuser-Busch, Inc.

---

12. http://www.herzlia.com/content/?ContentID=ce5cd613-ff1c-4d09-9082-1a81 dcb4d71f&Section=1
13. http://www.washingtonpost.com/wp-dyn/content/article/2008/06/21/AR2008062 101825.html?nav=rss_print/asection
14. http://www.allbusiness.com/retail-trade/miscellaneous-retail/4433726-1.html
15. http://www.bestplacestoworkinpa.com/bestplaces.asp

Endnotes

About the Author

Susan Stamm is the president of The TEAM Approach®, a team development firm dedicated to helping people play nicer at work for the mutual benefit and profit of all. She believes that relationships are the key ingredient to happiness and success, personally, professionally, and globally. As host of the monthly "Bookends" teleconference and podcast, Stamm interviews authors of great books written for leaders, and HRD professionals, to discover their implications for today's workplace.

Stamm claims she has been a student of human behavior ever since her high school psychology course and is fascinated with how people transfer learning into consistent performance on the job. Susan is a co-creator of the "Team Leader Café," a radical approach to team leader development, which guarantees permanent measurable performance improvements for supervisors and team leaders. Susan enjoys classroom facilitation, and speaking or writing about workplace performance issues. She is especially motivated to help people put what they learn into action and feels training that does not support a transfer back to the job is a waste of everyone's time and resources.

Susan has an Associate of Applied Science's degree in Human Services from Delaware Technical and Community College and a Bachelor of Science degree in Management and Organizational Development from Eastern Mennonite University where she earned an Outstanding Achievement Award. She was a contributing author to the book: "10: The Top Tens of Employee Engagement" edited by David Zinger. Additionally, Susan serves on the advisory boards for Vital Learning Corporation and Performance Support Systems. A member of American Society of Training and Development (ASTD) National, and the Central Pennsylvania Chapter of ASTD, she also cohosts the monthly Red Rose Learning Community gatherings in Lancaster, Pennsylvania. Susan is married to her best friend, Rick Stamm, and has three children: Rachel, Adam, and Sarah, and three grandchildren: Bryan, Dylan, and Anna.

Recommended Super Star Press® Books

Purchase these books at Happy About
http://www.happyabout.com
or at other online and physical bookstores.

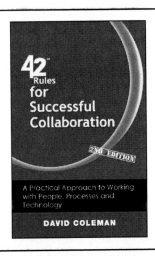

42 Rules of Successful Collaboration

This book helps the readers to walk away with a much better idea on how to be successful in their interactions with others via the computer.

Paperback: $19.95
eBook (pdf): $14.95

Blitz the Ladder

Unique approach to improve your career 'Blitz the Ladder' will provide you an in-depth view at a unique approach to improving your career.

Paperback: $19.95
eBook (pdf): $14.95

A Message from Super Star Press™

Thank you for your purchase of this 42 Rules Series book. It is available online at: http://www.happyabout.com/42rules/employee-engagement.php or at other online and physical bookstores. To learn more about contributing to books in the 42 Rules series, check out http://superstarpress.com.

Please contact us for quantity discounts at sales@superstarpress.com.

If you want to be informed by email of upcoming books, please email bookupdate@superstarpress.com.

CPSIA information can be obtained at www.ICGtesting.com
Printed in the USA
BVOW02s0044150516

447944BV00004B/5/P